How to create a new
Vegetable
Garden

How to create a new
Vegetable
Garden

Producing a beautiful and
fruitful garden from scratch

Charles Dowding

Published by

Green Books
An imprint of UIT Cambridge Ltd
www.greenbooks.co.uk

PO Box 145, Cambridge CB4 1GQ, England
+44 (0)1223 302 041

First published in 2015, in England

Charles Dowding has asserted his moral rights under the
Copyright, Designs and Patents Act 1988.

Front cover photograph: iStockphoto
Back cover photographs: Charles Dowding / Naomi Schillinger

All interior photographs, with the exception of those listed below, are
by the author and Steph Hafferty. Except for those on pages 8, 54-5,
172 and 232, all interior photographs show the author's
garden in its first year.
Page 7: *Which? Gardening.* Pages 21, 112, 158 & 203: Shutterstock.

Design by Jayne Jones

ISBN: 978 0 85784 244 2 (hardback)
ISBN: 978 0 85784 245 9 (ePub)
ISBN: 978 0 85784 246 6 (pdf)
Also available for Kindle

10 9 8 7 6 5 4 3 2 1

Contents

To Steph, whose help at Homeacres
has been fantastic.

Acknowledgements

Thanks to Robin Baxter and Christina for help at key moments; and to Mick Denney, so practical and encouraging. Thanks to Darren McGrath, who got to know my bindweed; to Hiro and Ken, Josh Rogers, George Oram and Jenny Jackson; and to Alethea Doran, for so many helpful suggestions with the writing.

Foreword

As the veg specialist on *Which? Gardening*, when offering advice to readers, I found that the hardest question to answer was "I want to grow vegetables; how do I start?" I've started three allotments myself over the years, and watched many novices start out enthusiastically but fail to make a go of it. This book would surely have made a difference. How many of us set out with good intentions and a head full of what we want to grow, while ignoring the key to success – getting the soil right?

Charles has had years of experience growing his own veg (not forgetting fruit and ornamentals), and his advice is founded on his experimental approach to growing, which is the real strength of his latest book. It doesn't just provide advice on starting your own veg plot but also documents in detail the first year in his own new garden. If there are alternative techniques for clearing land and building fertility, you can be sure Charles has tried them – as you would expect of a teacher and experimenter. Rather than the 'trust me, I am an expert' approach, this book modestly lays out the evidence for the merits of each technique, so readers can see for themselves and decide which methods suit them best.

The second part of the book gives details of all the vegetables, arranged by season, that you might wish to grow; written in an honest and informative style by someone who really has grown them all, over many years. Not only that, but it offers advice on how to optimize the harvest from a smaller space over a season.

Charles is well known for his advocacy of no-dig gardening. I met him while researching a feature on digging versus no-dig. He convinced me, and I have been practising it on my own allotment ever since. I hope he will convince you too.

Steve Mercer

Steve Mercer spent 30 years researching and writing for *Which? Gardening* magazine. Now retired, he is devoting more time to his garden and allotments.

Introduction

This book is about how to make a new garden, however unpromising the starting point may seem. While it is mostly about growing vegetables, it covers ornamental plants too – and challenges any idea that a veg garden may not also be a beautiful garden. There is advice on cutting, clearing, levelling and mulching to have clean soil for planting – quickly and easily sometimes; more slowly at other times – according to what you are starting with and what you want to achieve.

I have gone through this process myself several times over the last three decades, and draw on this experience to describe a range of short cuts that can be used for clearing ground: particularly the use of light-excluding mulches to kill persistent weeds, and leaving the soil undisturbed. You can see how the different ways of mulching work from the photos in this book, which show the transformation of my new garden of Homeacres over the course of its first year. As well as giving detailed accounts of these methods so that beginners can apply them easily, I explain the underlying principles, in order that experienced gardeners can work with them in varied situations.

There are several overlapping themes running through the book:
- Labour-saving methods for clearing weedy spaces.
- Ways to make the soil more fertile, for healthier growth in a smaller space and fewer weeds.
- Specific advice on vegetable growing, including propagation, sowing times and harvesting – for growing outside, in polytunnels or green-houses, and in hot beds.
- How to make and maintain a beautiful garden, including when it is mainly for food.

A key principle underpinning the methods described in this book is that you don't need to dig and cultivate soil. As well as being quicker initially, this reduces the subsequent workload, because undisturbed soil germinates fewer weed seeds.

However you do it, the first year in a new garden is busier than subsequent ones, and I would urge you to find as much time as possible to spend on it during the first months, especially when there are perennial weeds to deal with. Mulching to kill otherwise-persistent weeds saves so much time in subsequent years, enabling you to be more creative.

Beauty is important, and so I suggest ideas for keeping a productive area looking attractive, through planting and careful maintenance of food and ornamental plants, which will all be blooming because the soil is

Left: My front garden in its second summer. Just 18 months earlier it was a wilderness (see page 38).

healthy. The examples of making flower beds and lawns have the same underlying theme as for making vegetable beds: of low maintenance, after thorough preparation.

Harnessing natural processes and experimenting

Gardening is most successful when you can replicate the natural processes in the environment of your area. Applying compost to the soil surface, for example, copies the way in which recycling works in nature, but is also boosted by the head start from the compost heap. In the UK, where conditions are often damp, a mulch of well-decomposed compost feeds the soil and protects the surface from the weather, without encouraging slugs. In drier climates, it is more appropriate to use mulches of less decomposed materials, as there they can break down in situ without a slug problem developing.

I have gardened no-dig and organically since 1983, using these methods in market gardens ranging in size from a quarter of an acre to seven acres, with ornamental areas and fruit-growing too. Organic, no-dig growing is a natural system and is not complicated, the main ingredients being compost, time and an observant nature.

Curiosity is a great thing for a gardener, and it is fascinating to try out different ways of preparing soil and growing plants. A variety of experiments are described in these pages, ranging from the use of different materials for mulching weeds and composts, and for different lengths of time, to comparisons between digging and not digging, and even trying not using compost at all. I have tested many ways of clearing weeds, making beds and extending the seasons to grow food, and explain them here.

I hope you can use the results of these experiments to give you ideas for your own garden. Having a go at new ways of growing makes it more interesting and exciting – then you are more likely to be successful, from being keenly involved and watching closely to observe growth.

My own new garden

I found myself at Homeacres during a time of personal upheaval and after leaving behind an established garden. It was a difficult time, but I was much helped by having a new garden to create. My partner Steph is a keen gardener too, and we enjoyed being creative at Homeacres whenever

she had time available from work and from her own home, garden and allotment. Most jobs go better when you can work together with someone. If you have friends who like gardening, sharing the load can work wonders for both of you. The early days at Homeacres were made much easier by other friends too, such as Robin from Nottingham, who made a great difference at that time.

When I arrived, in November 2012, Homeacres was a little wild. This arose partly from it having been a market garden in the 1960s and 1970s, which I discovered only after moving in. When the market gardener died, his relatives stayed on but left the greenhouses to fall down, their glass on the soil and masonry in it, and the site became overgrown with a forest of brambles until a decade ago. Thankfully, that had been cleared by previous owners, and my main inheritance of the market garden is lumps and paths of concrete, gravel and glass in the soil, from the old greenhouses and sheds.

Apart from the debris, I was happy to discover that the place had been a market garden, which suggested a soil of fair quality. When Steph and I first looked at the house, the previous August, I brought along a spade to dig a small hole in the pasture, to see how the soil looked. The estate agent remarked that she had never seen a house buyer do that, and I was happy after finding some crumbly soil on a level site. This decided me to make an offer for the property, although from a gardening point of view it

Late June – just 4-5 months after these beds were made.

looked sorrowful at the time. Selling produce was not my intention at Homeacres, where I saw a new garden as the backdrop for teaching, writing and playing with ideas for clearing and growing that I wanted to compare. Then one day in early April I stood back and saw that the number of new beds had become more than I originally envisaged. As I hesitated with a tray of lettuce plants in my hand, and with Steph's encouragement, I decided to make the first plantings for eventual sales.

The garden now has several roles, from educational and experimental to ornamental and productive. As well as making space for vegetables, I have cleared and planted beds of flowers, fruit trees and bushes, so the garden is a pleasure to behold as well as providing plenty to eat. Its productivity has led me back into selling salads to local shops and restaurants, and some weekly boxes of vegetables. I have also enjoyed assembling a weekly crate of vegetables for a local restaurant, The Pilgrims Rest at Lovington, whose chef Jules is keen on using tasty, colourful vegetables as part of the main dish, rather than as a garnish.

How to use this book

The book is in two parts: the first on clearing ground and preparing soil; the second on sowing and growing. Although they overlap, in that you can sow and plant straight away into a freshly filled bed, with all the weeds mouldering underneath, Part 1 is specifically about the time, resources and methods needed to create a productive garden. I take a close look at all the different ways of creating a clean surface, with results of several trials to compare the qualities of different mulch materials.

Part 2 starts with what to sow, at the best time and using different methods of sowing, all through the growing year. This is spread through three chapters, and then Chapter 12 ties it together with examples of sowings and harvests from one bed over a single season. The next two chapters offer advice on extending the growing season, both under cover and in hot beds, and finally I give some tips on growing perennial vegetables, to spread the workload and extend the season of harvests.

I hope this book gives you inspiration and encouragement for creating your own beautiful and bountiful garden – however daunting its beginnings may be.

A note on terminology

I want this book to be useful in many countries, so have included imperial measurements as well as metric, and, as far as possible, I describe the timing of jobs in a seasonal context as well as with reference to the times of year in the UK. For example, February is late winter and June is early summer; see the Appendix for full details.

The Glossary explains specific phrases and words used in this book which may not be familiar to some readers, and I trust that this will ensure that my meaning is clear throughout. Plenty of photos should help to put you in the picture!

A July box of Homeacres' vegetables for the Pilgrims Rest pub.

PART ONE

Clearing ground and preparing soil

CHAPTER ONE

Starting points

Formulating ideas and first steps

"Life begins the day you start a garden."

Chinese proverb

A garden grows with you, and the way that it evolves is a big part of the pleasure. Start small, nurture ideas, and develop some plans in your mind and also on paper. The main thing is to create a garden that matches your available time, because it is far more enjoyable to be always in control of growth, weeds in particular, than to be struggling to stay on top of things. It's important to keep an open mind about trying some different approaches

Top: In January, I am sinking and sliding in the cold mud. Bottom: By September, without any soil cultivations, the garden is blooming.

as the garden grows, and I recommend that you read the first chapters of this book before becoming too involved! This chapter offers some guidance about where to start and how to manage your plans, with an example of my first project in the new garden.

How much garden you can manage depends on how you set it up, what you grow, how much time you can give and also your level of fitness. The last improves with gardening – an absorbing hobby which can draw you into doing more.

The first few months are key in clearing space: according to what you find there may be stones and rubble to clear, vigorous weeds to mulch and overgrown trees and bushes to cut back, as described in Chapters 3 and 4. This is an intensive phase of garden creation, before things settle down.

One way in which growing vegetables differs from growing ornamentals is in the extra time needed to harvest and prepare or store produce. Then after that there is ground to be cleared before starting again, often replanting the same space twice in a season. Intensively planted, smaller areas can be as productive as weedier and less well-tended larger areas. So, for a busy person, it is worth considering starting with just one bed.

Starting out at Homeacres I had occasional help from Steph and friends, and some help later with harvesting salads, but mainly the labour is my own, on a plot of three-quarters of an acre. It is not full-time, as I have other commitments. The labour-saving methods I explain in this book make it possible to garden a larger area in less time than would otherwise be possible.

To design or not

Everything is achievable, and it's a big help to mull things over while your feet are, literally, on the ground: imagine some ideas while out there, not just by looking at a plan on paper. Even if you have little experience, nothing beats making pictures in the head, while in the garden. Put an imaginary greenhouse right there and then see with your mind's eye if it would be easy to access, how it would look and how it might relate to the rest of your garden. Nurture the ideas you have and sketch them out as a temporary framework or guideline, just in a rough way. Then be prepared as things manifest to alter any bit that feels wrong or impractical. You will find that new and exciting ideas can pop up while actually gardening, which is a highly creative process.

November 2012: first steps – removing a wooden fence.

I found that Homeacres daunted me with its overgrown aspect – there seemed too much that I needed to do. Ideas for a new garden were bubbling in the background, but they felt nebulous and uncertain at that stage.

Somehow I needed to have a garden running by next spring, as a base for courses, writing and visits by groups keen to learn. What might I show them?

As it turned out, the answer was "A lot", for example the many possible ways to clear ground, clean soil, create a growing space and have harvests in a short time period. If you like working to a plan, I suggest having one with a 't' on the end – a growing plan that can change and adapt to weather, weeds and growth as it happens.

Time, energy, health

A bold and beautiful plan is useless unless you can give it the necessary time and energy, or have the money to make time. You also need a commitment to turn your wishes into reality, so it is good to ask yourself "How much do I really want that?" A powerful "Very much" will help you somehow make it happen.

Gardening is a physical activity, and the more you do, the more your muscles respond with new energy after an initial tiredness. At first, doing a little regularly is important: keep going and then feel rewarded as your body strengthens, warms up and looks better too. Gardening improves your mental health too, especially in terms of the uplifting effects of working

Salad leaves – my main output from the garden.

physically outdoors, even in poor weather. Being outside in winter is a powerful tonic, allowing more light to your body at a time when it is particularly valuable for feeling in good spirit. Then you gain more health by eating the vibrant food you have grown. Thanks to all these factors I enjoyed good health while I was creating my garden at Homeacres and never missed a day, or even an hour, to ill health, throughout a wet winter and bitterly cold spring, all during my 55th year.

First jobs to tackle

If you have not gardened before, and are faced with an overgrown or bare or rubble-filled plot, don't give up at the discouraging outlook. On the other hand, don't imagine it finished in a day! Just tackle one thing at a time and keep at it, enjoying the sense of achieving each new job. This process of gradual progress is the underlying story here: taking one step at a time and taking heart from every one.

For example, at Homeacres I was itching to clear the brambles, because they were grabbing my trousers while I was moving furniture through the front door. The 'front garden' showed signs of having been beds and borders long ago, but these were covered with thorns, nettles, ivy, bindweed and other weeds of all kinds, in addition to a few once-ornamental bushes.

Initially I wasn't sure I wanted to commit time to creating much garden in the front, so we just did some basic clearance, mainly cutting back brambles and mowing the wilderness. This was a great start, even though the soil was still full of weed roots and stems. Shade was another issue, and many gardens have this overhanging problem. If the trees and hedges are yours and you want to grow food, I urge tight pruning if you want to keep them at all. You can also cut back to your neighbour's boundary any overgrowth such as ivy or honeysuckle.

I was bothered by a line of 9m (30')-high spruce trees on the south-west boundary, planted 40 years earlier to create a windbreak. They kept out the prevailing wind, but were very dark and slightly foreboding. The house was in shade from early afternoon in the winter months, and the conifer roots were pulling moisture and nutrients from an area I wished to grow on. So I booked a local farmer to cut them down as soon as he was free.

I was a little unsure of how my new neighbours would react to these trees coming down, and one afternoon a rather stern-looking woman walked up the drive while I was clearing brambles. She briefly introduced herself as a near neighbour and then said, "I hear you are having these trees cut down and I thought I should let you know that you are going to make a lot of people very . . . happy!" Apparently all the neighbours hated the shade, and I was so relieved. Increase the light coming into your garden as much as possible, and your house will feel more cheerful too.

Weather and climate

The weather and climate at your site are fundamental influences, so it is worth taking time to observe them, such as how much frost lies in the garden and how the wind comes in. Mark Twain said "Climate is what we expect; weather is what we get", but, in short, climate is the average weather conditions over a long period of time. This, more than anything else, affects what you can grow, and you will enjoy best harvests if you plant according to climate, rather than being tempted by exotic plants from distant areas. Look at what your neighbours are growing, especially those who have gardened for a while. Climate also affects sowing and harvesting dates, so check where any gardening advice is coming from to see if it is appropriate for your area.

The advice in this book is based on the conditions at Homeacres (see table below), which is in a climatic zone equivalent to zone 8 or 9 in the US system of plant hardiness zones. Here, it is often mild, cloudy and windy. The amount of sunlight is low relative to temperature, which is mild thanks to the Gulf Stream. Gusty south-west winds often blow off the Atlantic, where they have been warmed by the sea. Much of the time there is some wind from the ocean, which brings relative warmth, especially in winter. This makes it possible to grow, and also to garden more, in winter.

Winter footings

Apart from what to start with, another question is when to start. Winter is an oft-neglected season in which much can be achieved to make the rest of the year more successful. A good place to be in gardening is one step ahead, rather than one step behind. For example, when there is an unexpectedly warm spring it can feel as though you are running to catch up, unless you're well prepared. Start as soon as possible – there is no right or wrong time to begin those first jobs, but creating the bones of a garden in winter will give you more time to flesh it out in spring and summer.

The local climate at Homeacres*				
Mean temperature			Rainfall	Sunshine
Dec–Mar	Apr–May; Oct–Nov	Jun–Sep		
5.5°C (42°F)	9.8°C (50°F)	15.7°C (60°F)	788mm (31.0")	1,560 hours

*Data from a nearby meteorological station at Yeovilton in Somerset.

Late January: these beds were recently made, in wet and cold weather.

Watch the weather forecast and grab any chances to be out there on fine days in winter; even be willing to garden in unpromising conditions. Weather is often a constraint in gardening, and it's no good waiting for perfect conditions. I arrived at Homeacres during one of the wettest years on record, so the soil was saturated throughout the first months. However, a no-dig approach can continue in almost any weather, and you can certainly spread compost and mulches on soggy soils that could not be cultivated in any way, so I made a lot of new beds in those sodden months.

Sometimes it turned colder, which helped because frosty weather made the surface hard, giving better support to me and my wheelbarrow. By the end of February, I could already see a garden in the making.

The compost heap

Starting a compost heap is one of the first things to do in a new garden, as you will have plenty of waste material to put somewhere. You can then enjoy watching it turn into something really useful. You don't even need to give it special attention – lovely compost happens, even where no particular heat has been generated. Cool compost of high quality is made by fungi, rather than the bacteria that are active in hot compost heaps.

Enclosure or container?

In small gardens, an unobtrusive plastic 'hive' container is suitably compact and can be sited wherever is most convenient. *Which? Gardening* magazine

Building the first compost heap at Homeacres. **1.** First fill! December. **2.** By February the heap is nearly full, with some weeds growing out of the side. **3.** June, before turning – with grass mowings in the top layers. **4.** By October it is great stuff, but full of weed seeds.

did a trial of different compost bins, including proprietary ones, reported in their issue of May 2014, and found that in fact a wooden enclosure made the best compost, probably because it provided more exposure to air than plastic containers. You can spend a lot of money on rotating drums, but these were found to work poorly, apparently from lack of ventilation as much as anything. Their main virtue was being impenetrable to rats, and, unfortunately, even if you put no food in a compost heap, rats may live there in winter because of the warmth it gives. A good compromise is a plastic bin sitting on chicken wire on the soil, to exclude rodents, and the contents occasionally lifted and loosened with a proprietary spiked aerator.

Location and turning

In larger gardens, a central location for the compost heap has the advantage of giving access from all parts. Heaps can be 1-1.2m (3-4') square and enclosed with old pallets for their sides; I put mine against an existing fence for one side. Turning once, into a neighbouring bay, about a month after a heap's last fill, is an optional extra for quicker compost, and it is usually ready for use when 8-12 months old.

Weed roots and seeds

The first heap you make while clearing a garden is likely to contain more weed seeds than usual, from the soil on roots being full of them; I certainly found this to be true. An important point is that you can put all roots of brambles and perennial weeds, including bindweed, dock, couch grass and stinging nettles, on the compost heap: they add goodness and decompose well. Long-stemmed waste is best cut to 10cm (4") lengths for faster decomposition and easier spreading of compost.

My first compost heap at Homeacres, made from weeds including all the roots, kitchen waste, wood ash and some mown grass, was full by April after 5 months of gradual filling. I left it a while, then turned it into an adjoining enclosure in June, then by August it had become quite beautiful: soft and fine. In a container trial with four lettuce plants, this compost gave good growth compared with plants grown in cow manure, green-waste compost and multipurpose compost. The downside, however, was the huge number of grass and stinging nettle seeds in it (see Chapter 4, page 59).

Creating the first beds **My first gardening project** at Homeacres was to turn an old chicken run into beds for vegetables. The photographs overleaf illustrate how it unfolded. This is a good example of concentrating on creating one space for growing, in damp winter weather and quickly too. I was fortunate that there were only annual weeds in this area – mostly grasses, thistles and chickweed – and so most of the initial work was done in one weekend, in late November.

Clearing edges

Edges are important to keep tidy and a good place to start, so I removed the old wire fence and cut off a row of stinging nettles along its line, pulling out many of their roots, then I pruned back shrubby growth from my neighbour Gert's garden. He is a keen organic gardener and in just 6 years has created an oasis of trees, flowers and vegetables, full of birds, and some of the plants spill outwards.

Thick cardboard laid on pathways.

Two-year-old cow manure laid on top of weeds.

Mulching to clean soil and for planting

Creating a garden in the old chicken run was simpler than in the rest of Homeacres, thanks to the absence of vigorous perennial weeds (see Chapter 4, page 62) – so, for example, one layer of cardboard was enough to create clean paths.

I laid 60cm (2') strips of thick cardboard boxes, making three pathways 1.2m (4') apart, and then spread 10cm (4") of 2-year-old cow manure to make raised beds between the cardboard, without any sides.

Putting all the ingredients on top saves messing with potential problems underneath: in this case there is gravel and some clinker of coal ash, from when the boilers for heating greenhouses had been here 50 years ago. Also, there are occasional large paving slabs under the soil, which my dibber sometimes bounces off when making holes for planting, but the plants can root around them.

Salads planted into one bed (November).

Salads in February, after much frost.

July: beans on left; peas in middle; onions on right.

August: onions harvested; kale abundant.

Small time input, many harvests

The area measures 5m x 6m (16' x 20'), and needed 16 hours of time and 1½ tons of compost for this initial preparation, then through the first year it produced lovely harvests of onions, garlic, salads, beans, courgettes, kale and sweet peas.

   Growth has been healthy and weeds have been few, with occasional hoeings and hand weeding to keep the surface spotless. It helped that the cardboard was from removal boxes, so it was thick and lasted for a good length of time before decomposing in situ. I maintain the high fertility in these beds with a wheelbarrow of compost for each bed in the autumn or winter, whenever the ground is clear.

September: salads after peas; more kale after onions.

October: beans cleared; compost spreading.

CHAPTER TWO

Beauty in the food garden

A garden both ornamental and edible

"In a garden, making the veg space a place to linger is top priority for me."

Bunny Guinness, garden writer and designer

While a vegetable garden rarely boasts the year-round visual appeal of mixed ornamental plantings, there are ways to make it beautiful. You can make an attractive look by growing smaller annual flowers among vegetables, judicious planting of fruit trees along edges, creating flower borders where space allows, and regular maintenance of the garden to keep plants in good health – as well as the vibrancy that comes from soil being in good health. This chapter describes ways in which ornamental plants can be integrated with vegetables without compromising their growth, indeed sometimes improving it, and suggests planting ideas for a striking look with vegetables alone. It also includes examples of how I created flower beds and a grassed area at Homeacres, in a short space of time.

Specific needs of vegetables

A garden of flowering plants intermixed with food plants is possible but not easy, for the reasons described below. However, there can be beauty in a vegetable garden in every season. Even in winter you can have richly composted beds among vegetables of varied form and colour, from kale, leeks and salads to emerging seedlings of broad beans and garlic – appealing for their symmetry and a promise of harvests to come.

Growing together

I have tried plantings of vegetables with ornamentals in many ways, and find it more difficult than growing vegetables on their own, which germinate reliably in open space and grow best in fertile soil and in full light. For plentiful and reliable harvests I suggest two main principles:

- Keep the emphasis on vegetables, because they are more transitory and often need a decent amount of clear soil for new sowings and plantings, which is difficult if ornamental plants are in a majority.

California poppies and nasturtiums with peas.

- For an ornamental look to the food plot, grow annual rather than perennial flowers, to minimize the slug habitat of winter and spring leaves. Most of the flowers mentioned here are annuals.

Even without flowers, you can achieve an appealing look by mixing plants up a little, rather than dividing the plot into four quarters for the sake of rotation (see Chapter 11, page 170): the vegetables then look more informal and with pleasing contrasts of shape and palette. All through the season one is making new plantings anyway, which creates a dynamic effect.

Often a need to harvest and replant

The need for picking and replanting with vegetable growing is in major contrast to purely ornamental gardening, where many plantings are more permanent, giving shape and colour over many years. An equivalent approach in food gardening is to grow more perennial vegetables (see Chapter 15) and even to go a step further by making a forest garden (see Resources), such as by planting fruit trees among vegetables. This does change the menu, though, and for high productivity from small plots it is hard to do better than growing mainly annuals.

Everything here except parsnip is a second planting after summer harvests.

Fruit with vegetables

In theory, growing fruit trees among vegetables is a great way to increase productivity, and as well as fruit, you will enjoy some great blossom. However, there is no getting away from the demands of trees and bushes for moisture and nutrients, which reduces the growth of nearby plants to varying degrees, mostly in summer and autumn. Whether you can succeed with both fruit and vegetables in proximity depends on your climate and priorities for food.

Edible hedges

An excellent way to create structure, add beauty and have fruit in the food garden is by planting along its edges and near to compost heaps. Fruits such as grapes and Japanese wineberries (*Rubus phoenicolasius*) can be grown along fences or trellis, or you can grow plants such as Chilean guava (*Myrtus ugni*) individually or as a small hedge. There are many new fruiting plants becoming available, although few give as much fruit as the more traditional ones.

Chilean guava for a small, edible hedge.

Apples are reliable and productive in temperate climates, and I have found their roots less competitive with vegetables than those of other tree fruit. Look for trees on M9 or M27 rootstock, which are less vigorous and crop earlier too, from their second summer onwards. Trees on M27 are small enough to grow within a vegetable plot, while trees on M9 are better along an edge. You can train them to a range of linear shapes such as cordon and espalier. Detailed advice can be found in *The Fruit Tree Handbook* (see Resources).

Soft fruit

Fruit bushes add another element of structure, and can be interplanted with vegetables when young. However, by the third summer their roots will have filled much of the soil and they need most of the space, unless widely planted. Also, having them in a line or group together makes netting easier, and in many gardens this is vital to keep birds off the fruit.

Another point is that fruits such as raspberries are invasive, with suckering roots travelling a long distance. The most suitable fruit to grow as part of a vegetable garden is strawberries – but, again, be prepared to protect them from birds when fruiting (cloche hoops to support netting are simple and effective).

The allure of a food garden

It is fun to grow food plants in interesting ways, with a wide vista of ever-changing visual effects to enjoy. Every year you can have new growing (and culinary) adventures, with new flavours, exciting to anticipate, in every season.

Growing food for healthy eating goes hand in hand with creating a beautiful garden. How plants look reflects the soil quality and the care given, as well as the season, and vibrant growth suggests nutritious food. In lively soil, leaves take on a deep hue and exude well-being, with stronger and glossier growth. Even if mostly green, they vary in shape and colour, while fruits and roots are bigger and finer too.

The way that a garden reflects the care given to it is alluded to in sayings such as 'the best fertilizer is the gardener's shadow', and it's the same thing for farmers: 'the best manure is the farmer's foot'. You can create a virtuous circle, because the glow of healthy plants is like a pull that attracts you to be involved with them. Regular tending of the garden helps to keep it looking beautiful, because being there means you see and undertake the ongoing maintenance that is needed, such as weeding, tidying, staking and picking. To be a good gardener, the first step is always to be out there whenever possible, and this is more likely to happen when good-looking plants are calling you.

Planting patterns

Beauty is in the eye of the beholder, so there is no formula for creating a garden of universal acclaim: your layout and planting will be certainly different from those of your neighbours. The following suggestions give

Ruby chard provides a welcome splash of colour in November.

a few ideas for maintaining a pleasing effect at all times of the year.

Aim high. Have really clean soil around your plants, and see how this makes everything look more attractive. Be conscientious with weeding, so that the varied forms and colours of vegetables and flowers are framed by and stand out against clean soil, with any outer edges, of both beds and the plot as a whole, kept neat as well.

Straight or curvy lines? The choice is yours, but straight lines are easier to manage and to access, and look nice when soil and plants are in good health. Curvy leaves and varying plant forms soften the straightness of planting lines.

On larger plots, you can improve plant health by mixing up plants from different families, especially those of which you grow a lot. Having blocks of varied vegetables in different beds helps reduce the risk of pests cleaning up in one go, and also creates an appealing patchwork effect in the garden. Furthermore, planting in blocks rather than having individual plants dotted around creates a striking look, for both flowers and vegetables. Beds planted with groups of broad beans, carrots, beetroot, lettuce and cabbages, for example, create pleasing visual contrasts, which also change as the season progresses.

Edible flowers

Colour in the garden can also be ornament on the plate. Flowers of nasturtium (*Tropaeolum* spp.), pot marigold (*Calendula officinalis*), borage (*Borago officinalis*), pansies (*Viola* spp.), cornflower (*Centaurea cyanus*), day lilies (*Hemerocallis* spp.) and mallows (*Malva* spp.) are edible. They

Autumn salads (mustards and salad rocket) planted early September.

won't fill you up, but are great for garnishing, while leaves such as nasturtium are edible too. Many herbs also have edible flowers, for example chives, chervil, oregano, thyme and basil; as do many vegetables, including peas and all brassicas, especially mustards for a really pungent flavour. Even some common wild flowers are good to eat, for example dandelions and daisies.

Friendly flowers for vegetables

One way to deter pests is to grow 'companion plants' among your vegetables. For example, marigolds help to keep whitefly off tomatoes, because their smell is a deterrent to aphids. However, this is not a method for pest-free gardening – which is a good thing, because if all the pests are gone there will be fewer predators on hand for maintaining a balance when new pests fly in.

A continuing but small number of pests, kept in check by some predators, is a sensible aim, and planting flowers helps, as they attract different insects. I don't think anyone knows the precise combinations of which flower attracts which pest and/or predator, in different conditions, so here is a simple rule of thumb. Plant the flowers you enjoy, just as long as they are not too large. Those that I have found to grow well with vegetables include snapdragons (*Antirrhinum* spp.), gladioli (*Gladiolus* spp.), verbena of different kinds (*Verbena* spp.), pansies, trailing lobelia (*Lobelia erinus*), annual flax (*Linum grandiflorum*), California poppy (*Eschscholzia californica*) and marigolds of all varieties except the 2m (6'6") *Tagetes minuta*.* Save

Tagetes minuta is claimed to repel couch grass and ground elder, but I have not succeeded with it, finding the couch grass as strong as ever around the tall marigolds.

A single plant of nasturtium 'Alaska' (front left) for salad leaves and flowers.

the taller, hungry cosmos and sunflowers for separate borders.

Growing flowers among your vegetables creates vibrant patches of strong colour among the edible plants, and, if for no other reason, they are valuable because the effect looks wonderful. It works well to plant flowers at bed ends, where they spill on to pathways and give a nice touch to the plot.

Creating new beds of annual flowers

Of course, any spare parts of a garden can be made into beds for flowers. On the following pages are three examples from my Homeacres garden. Each had different histories and illustrate different ways to prepare soil and to sow or plant, according to the soil and weeds you have to deal with.

Many annual flowers grow pleasingly fast from sowing direct into the soil, as long as you wait until the days are warming up – a fortnight or even a month after the spring equinox. On the other hand, raising plants in pots or modules and planting them out when they are a more robust size makes for easier weeding around them, and it's also easier to achieve precise patterns of form and colour this way, as you can set out a few plants here and there – with direct sowing the results are less predictable.

I use the same methods for growing flowers as for vegetables, that is, adding a layer of compost on top of undisturbed soil. The compost serves as a weed-suppressing mulch, is easier to hoe and to pull weeds out of than soil, and gives flowering plants healthy colour with abundant growth. A layer of just 1cm (½") makes a worthwhile difference.

Conservatory bed

If your new garden has recently been a building site, you are likely to be faced with a sticky mess, even if the builders have covered the compacted working area with what may pass for topsoil. Commercial topsoil is extremely variable and often difficult to work into any kind of easily maintained surface. This was the story at Homeacres, where the area beside my conservatory became a muddy mess in late winter, its soil squashed to a puddle by a dumper truck, and with large pieces of concrete (the foundations of an old greenhouse) embedded in it.

My friend Robin was down for the weekend and we levered out massive lumps of the concrete with a crowbar. If he had not been there, I would have had to leave them under the surface, because some of the pieces were huge and heavy. Extracting them resulted in a slightly sunken area relative to the adjoining mud, where I planned to sow grass (see page 41). At one end there were some dandelion and couch grass roots, but at the other the mud was mostly clear of growth, squashed by builders' machinery.

I filled the sunken area with 10cm (4") of 2-year-old manure, good for planting into and easy to weed. The few existing weeds were thus well covered, and through the summer I used a trowel to lever out occasional regrowth of couch grass and dandelion.

The right planting times for summer colour depend on spring weather, and may be as early as April or as late as June. In this case it was early May before I planted sweet peas (*Lathyrus odoratus*) around a wigwam of hazel supports, and California poppies and phlox (*Phlox paniculata*), then I filled the bed during the following month

With Robin, breaking concrete to remove it.

April: bed made with compost on top.

By July there is an abundance of flowers.

with module-raised plants, including gentian sage (*Salvia patens*), rudbeckia (*Rudbeckia herta*) and two medium-sized orange sunflowers (*Helianthus* spp.) in the middle of each half. Thanks to some watering in summer, the sweet peas continued flowering until September, in the midst of a glorious mass of colour.

Front border

The part of my front garden by the road was a desperately weedy area of old ornamental plantings, which I managed to ignore in the first few months, when it was simply a job too far. It had just a simple tidy-up in late autumn, when I dug out some woody brambles, pulled out most of the ivy, and mowed off some dense clumps of grass with fat leaves. Then, in the depths of a wet winter, a lorry containing a 10-ton load of compost that I had ordered could not reach the area I intended for it, and was obliged to drop its load near the road and on top of this weedy old border. The deep heap turned out to be a good mulch! Ten weeks later, after I'd spread the last barrowload of compost, there was only bindweed, a few brambles and some of the grass clumps, which I dug out. There were still weeds around two sides where the compost had not covered, so I laid thick cardboard on one and polythene on another, to await planting the following year.

All that remained was to plant into a clean surface on which I had left 5cm (2") of the compost, resulting in a reasonably weed-free bed all summer. Plantings included cosmos (*Cosmos* spp.), roses (*Rosa* spp.), clary sage (*Salvia sclarea*) and cornflowers (*Centaurea* spp.); they were nicely offset by catmint (*Nepeta cataria*), which sprang up near the road, and a peony (*Paeonia* spp.) at the other end. (See photo on page 8.) Throughout the summer I was still obliged to be there every few days with a trowel, levering out the hedge bindweed, until by September it had become smaller and infrequent.

November, after first cutting of the wilderness.

A daunting selection of weeds to clear.

February: compost landing on top of a weedy bed.

June: polythene mulch over weeds where no compost.

July: new plantings and existing catmint.

October: clean soil – even the bindweed is nearly gone.

Bonfire bed

Fire is one way to clear weeds thoroughly. After having the old conifer windbreak felled, I had a bonfire of the leaves and twigs, and then made a round 'bonfire bed' on the area. I scattered the bonfire ash and charcoal in the polytunnel and on a couple of new beds, leaving bare and clean soil behind. Then in late winter I spread about 7cm (3") of home-made and municipal compost on top of this soil, which was completely clean of weeds and looked rather barren.

Into this crumbly compost I sowed three rows of mixed annual flower seeds in early spring, 30cm (12") apart, and then set out random plants through the next 2 months until the summer solstice. I wanted a happy mixture of flowers. I had chosen a selection of flowers likely to grow well in this climate – many of the ones already mentioned (see pages 34-5), as well as blue vervain (*Verbena hastata*) and

March: spreading compost on the bonfire site.

July: phlox, snapdragons, poppies and California poppies.

nigellas (*Nigella damascena*) both blue and white. I sowed seed or pricked seedlings into modules in the greenhouse, similar to propagating vegetable plants. From early summer there was an explosion of colour, with only occasional weeding needed, and some dead-heading from midsummer onwards.

Sowing grass

You can sow grass at any time of year when there is moisture at the surface; sometimes even in summer if it's wet, but normally in the autumn and early spring months. Grass grows so easily in any climate with sufficient moisture, and is invasive where any edge meets bare soil. It needs regular maintenance and edging, so in a small garden you may be better with some hard standing, paving stones, gravel, shrubs or small trees to frame your ornamentals and edibles and make more use of limited space.

Grass mowings combine well in compost heaps with other garden waste, or you can mulch the grass with them, using a suitable mower – one that chops the grass finely enough that it quickly decays on the surface. Around the edges of my main plot and beds I mow every week to 10 days, to reduce slug habitat and inward creeping of the grass, and prevent any grass or weeds from seeding on to nearby soil.

For the perfect sward, some cultivation may be needed, but in most cases it is sufficient to simply level the surface. In damp climates, grass just wants to grow, on any soil – and it improves the soil structure all the time, with a dense mat of fine, spreading roots which encourage soil life and worms. The following example from Homeacres shows how willingly it grows.

Creating a lawn

In January, the soil where I wanted to sow grass was sticky and compacted: puddled by a dumper truck and covered with lying water. I waited for drier weather in March and then used a spade to remove larger stones and level off the main humps.

By April the surface was dry enough that no soil stuck to the boots, but was still damp underneath. I walked over the whole area to break up larger clods with my feet and then scattered grass seed, without raking it in.

The recommended sowing rate for grass seed to make a lawn is around 40g per square metre (1½oz per square yard), but I sowed at about a tenth of this rate and growth was fine, although a little thin.

On top of the sown ground, I spread barely 1cm (½") of municipal compost, walked over the whole area again to press the seed in, and waited for enough rain to start the grass growing.

In fact it rained 62mm (2½") during the next 4 weeks – enough for the grass to germinate and establish before summer, and from the middle of June it needed mowing. It was simple to transform ugly mud into average-looking green sward, with minimal input of time and materials. Using turf would have been more expensive, taken far longer and would also have entailed extra watering to make sure the turves settled in to growth, without drying out and going yellow.

February: mud after the dumper truck.

April: soil levelled, grass sown and compost spread.

July, and the grass is established.

CHAPTER THREE

The setting

Soil, shade, wind and pests

*"A gentle breeze is
nothing without the sound
of it blowing through
the leaves."*

Helene Pizzi, gardener and writer

Like the stage of a play, a garden's setting and qualities
influence how the plants can perform. Many factors
can be improved, while a few are immutable. This
chapter takes a look at some of the most important
ones, especially soil and the many ways in which
it influences what can grow. The examples from
Homeacres illustrate how you can change some, such
as trees and edges, and adapt to others, such as the
local wildlife, when creating a new garden.

Soil: drainage, moisture and fertility

Soil is the earth's skin of weathered rocks and plant materials. It is alive and more or less biologically active, depending on the climate, parent rocks and the local ecology. Soil affects everything in the garden and, since we cannot change its basic type, a good first step is to know the qualities of the soil you have. All soils have benefits to appreciate and make the most of, and disadvantages that you can reduce.

The table opposite describes the characteristics of each type of soil across a spectrum from heavy (clay) to light (sand), between which are silt, loam and chalk. A further possibility is 'builders' soil', since many new gardens are on soil corrupted by building work.

These categories are broad-brush definitions, and many soils are borderline between two types. For example, clay soils range from dense and yellow to less dense and browner, with some silty and loamy characteristics. Most loams have some sand, some silt and some clay. Homeacres is a clay loam, and within the garden it varies considerably.

There are two main principles to observe when setting out to improve soil, and these underpin the examples given in the rest of this book:

- First, disturb the soil as little as possible, to preserve its structure.
- Second, feed soil life with organic matter such as compost on the surface, to encourage the myriad organisms to multiply and be more active. This also further improves the soil structure. The soil organisms do a better job of aerating soil than we can, with more enduring effect, and fewer weeds as a result. Adding a surface layer of organic matter also helps to retain moisture.

Left: The profile of the trench for building the conservatory – shows dark loam over clay.
Right: Surface loam – shows how after frost you can make a tilth by knocking clods.

Characteristics and management of different soils				
Soil type	Texture	Moisture/drainage	Fertility	Approach
Clay	Some surface crumbs, sticky below	Holds moisture in summer, sticky in winter	Holds more nutrients than other soils	Rarely needs a first dig, surface composting ideal
Silt	Soft, dense but crumbly too	Holds moisture & drains too	Good, helped by physical quality	As for loam, but it dries out more slowly
Loam	Soft, crumbly	Holds some moisture & drains well	Reasonably fertile	Easy in all seasons, just surface compost
Chalk	Crumbly with chalk fragments	Free-draining, holds little moisture	Reasonably fertile	Extra compost to retain moisture & balance high pH
Sand	Grainy, even fluffy	Dries out quickly	Often poor, nutrients wash through	Compost in spring, for nutrients & to retain moisture
Builders' soil	Messy, sticky, perhaps stony, few worms	Variable but often lies wet & lacking air	May be poor, lacking organic matter	Initial dig to remove debris, then surface compost

On sandy soils, it is almost impossible to grow decent moisture-loving plants such as celery and celeriac, except in a continuously wet summer, and brassicas do not grow as big as they do on heavy soil. This disadvantage is balanced by the fact that most root vegetables, carrots in particular, grow well in light soil and are easy to harvest, with a cleaner surface.

At the other end of this spectrum, the ability of clay soil to hold more nutrients ensures the strong growth of most plants. However, there may be problems of drainage and water lying on the surface, especially in winter, so it is worth creating slightly raised beds where roots can survive above the water level in wet weather. In some low-lying spots, it may not be possible to overwinter vegetables such as garlic and parsnips; instead, plant the former in spring and harvest the latter in autumn.

A final factor, which sometimes affects what you can grow, is pH – the acidity or alkalinity of your soil. Most soils are somewhere between 6.0 and 7.5: more or less neutral. It is worth asking neighbours whether they have any issues in their gardens, because pH is similar over wide areas. A pH below 6.0 means acid soil, where brassicas will struggle, but potatoes will be fine and you can grow great blueberries. Adding some lime, in winter, raises pH, but in most soils this is not needed. Chalk soils have a high pH (alkaline), which may cause a lock-up of iron, but the addition of compost will improve nutrient flow.

Compacted soil

Soil is naturally firm and rarely needs any intervention to introduce air and improve drainage: firm soil is good for plants, having a stable matrix of air channels and providing a strong anchor to roots. The time to worry about compaction is after building work and any passage of heavy machinery in wet conditions. Loosening is best done with a sturdy garden fork, inserting it and levering gently: for this to succeed, soil needs to be at least half-dry and not sticky, so that the fork prongs have a slight shattering effect. It is important to only loosen the soil rather than to invert it, in order to preserve the natural gradient between topsoil and subsoil. However, I have found that surface compost and time – say a year or so of variable weather and worms burrowing – usually serves to restore soil health without any need for this.

Surface compaction caused by tractor wheels in wet conditions.

Stones

Large rocks and boulders need removing, but smaller stones are too numerous to clear, and common stones such as limestone offer moisture and minerals to plant roots. This is one of the advantages of a no-dig approach: it reduces any difficulty of working stony soil by leaving the stones buried, although soil freezing tends to ease stones upwards.

Access and slope

The ease of access and the gradient of a site are often linked: level sites with vehicular access are ideal, but I have seen many steep and successful gardens, even where access is restricted. Sometimes, for bringing in compost, the only method is by wheelbarrow or even hauling bags in, and some allotmenteers have to do this, finding they can move a surprising amount on a 'little and often' basis. I help Steph bring compost into her garden up some steep steps, by filling a wheelbarrow half-full and pulling it upwards, one step at a time.

I once came across a beautiful market garden in Devon, on a steep, south-facing slope, where a digger had scraped out soil and rock to create three wide, flat terraces, separated by steep banks with earth steps cut into them. It was an otherwise impossible slope, but now it worked well, with growth being early thanks to a south-westerly aspect. Dan the gardener had simply put two inches of compost on top of the reinstated topsoil, so keeping plants healthy and weeds to a minimum.

The site at Homeacres

Starting a new garden does have an aura of adventure, but with more uncertainties than in the garden's subsequent years. At Homeacres I had found a level, compact site, and this made everything easier. A local farmer's tractor and trailer dropped well-decomposed manure in four convenient places, before any beds were made, and the lack of slope made it easier to push a wheelbarrow than in any other garden I had worked on.

The heavy soil felt boggy in that first, wet winter. However, I continued to make raised beds, when soil cultivations of any kind were absolutely impossible. And using a wheelbarrow, rather than heavy machinery, allowed me to move compost around with minimal damage to the soil below.

Trees and hedges

For plants and especially vegetables to grow well, they need as much sun as possible, and sufficient moisture in summer. Trees and hedges take light and their roots take moisture – easy to overlook as they are out of sight, but travelling far horizontally. It is a myth that plant roots are a mirror image of their branches and stems, because most rooting happens near the surface, where soil is full of food, moisture and air.

Trees affecting light and moisture

Losing moisture and food to the trees was one reason I wanted to be rid of Homeacres' tall spruce windbreak, whose cutting is described in Chapter 1. A second reason was because the darkness of conifers is more solid than deciduous trees and so they felt foreboding too, even when the wind made music in their branches.

Deciduous trees and hedges are less invasive than evergreens, and pruning is often sufficient to make their impact manageable. On the southern boundary of Homeacres is a tall Bramley apple tree, and this was a mass of thick, crossing branches, as well as some lovely mistletoe, a sign of mild summers.* My main concern is when trees either cause shade or are robbing other plants of moisture in summer, and this one was doing

*Common mistletoe (Viscum alba) needs average summer temperatures above 16°C (61°F), which is common in southern Britain, but not in the north.

Apple trees planted near the hedge grew slowly.

both. So with the tree still dormant in late winter I took a chainsaw to the overlapping branches, removing half of them. This let more light in and gave higher-quality apples. It also reduced the amount of moisture needed by the tree, though some was still drawn in summer from the newly created beds of vegetables.

Hedges affecting light and moisture

Hedges are best pruned as tight as you dare. This not only reduces their demand for light and soil moisture but also makes their regrowth attractive, with lots of new greenery and less empty wood in the middle and at the bottom. Established hedge plants such as blackthorn, elder and hawthorn can be cut to just 1m (3') high and wide if you want, usually in winter but summer is fine too, once the birds' nesting season is finished. You can take the opportunity to cut or dig out any hedge brambles while pruning, as they otherwise keep invading.

Exposure to wind

Does the sheltering benefit of trees and hedges outweigh the drawback of their demands on resources? The answer depends on where you are. If you're beside the sea, for example, a shelter belt is valuable: trees filter wind in a better way than solid shelters such as walls and fences, because these cause turbulence.

After having the conifers cut down I am more exposed to the prevailing south-west and west winds. Yet my vegetables and flowers cope well and are helped by better light. In a garden exposed to wind, you need to stake some taller plants, use stronger poles for climbing beans and be thorough in securing cloches and plant covers.

I have planted a row of apple trees on M26 rootstock, in a line close to where the conifers were. M26 grows trees of medium size, up to 3.5m (11'6") – much larger than M27, which is for planting in smaller and sheltered spaces. They will not make a significant windbreak but will reduce the wind a little, with the benefit of fruit too, and they are less demanding of light, moisture and food than tall evergreens.

Young trees grow better in weed-free soil, so after planting we put a 10cm (4") mulch of horse manure and green-waste compost on top, to smother existing grass and weeds around the trees. Then I laid landscape

Maiden apple trees planted in winter were well established by August, with squash growing between them.

fabric (non-woven; see Chapter 5, page 74) on top, pushed into the soil with a spade to keep the edge at bay. In June I put one 'Uchiki Kuri' squash plant between each tree: these gave more value to the bed, and looked pretty too as the squash ripened deep orange, yielding four per plant.

Edges

While attention generally focuses on the middle of gardens, their edges often require more maintenance, be they hedge, fence, weeds or trees. Any grass edge against bare soil needs constant trimming and cutting back, so creating low-maintenance edges can save a lot of time, although this is not always possible. The front-garden boundary at Homeacres has a neighbour's overgrown border on its other side, with plants such as ivy, bindweed, brambles and Chinese lantern (*Physalis alkekengi*) invading under the fence panels. These rather spoil the success of mulches on my side, which have made the surface clean until the neighbour's perennial weeds arrive, and keep arriving.

For growing spaces within your own garden, you can reduce the amount of edge by having square or circular plots rather than long and thin ones. Sometimes a thin strip is unavoidable, as in my long bed of apple trees. Using a sharp spade or edging tool every 2-4 weeks in summer, to cut grass and weeds back, is often necessary.

A line of overlapping pieces of cardboard, 30-40cm (12-16") wide, can be laid around an area of vegetables to kill weeds initially and then to prevent them reinvading, especially in the case of couch grass. Along

A mulch of cardboard and land-scape fabric, with apple trees just planted.

these edges I run a rotary mower slightly over the top of the cardboard, so the blades can scoop up any overgrowing grass.

Wildlife

Any prevalence of wild animals can influence the fencing you need, and some animals are difficult to keep out. When moving to a new garden it is worth asking neighbours what animal problems they may have.

One example of an almost insoluble problem is urban foxes.

In my rural area I was discouraged to hear of badgers, deer and rabbits being a general problem. My garden is too large to fence against them, and I had already discovered the difficulties of keeping determined animals at bay. On one occasion, after I had dug in a fence all around a garden, badgers simply walked in through a front gate that had been left open. Laying covers over beds of vegetables was the most effective solution, using fleece* in spring and bird netting or mesh thereafter – these protect against every potential problem except large animals. Rabbits are especially fond of young plants, and new plantings of salads, chard, brassicas, carrots and leeks in particular need protection. I was worried by the appearance of badgers in midsummer, digging deep holes in some beds and ripping through fabric mulches: they are powerful animals. It transpired that they had mostly been drawn to eat my neighbour Gert's strawberries, and after trashing his bed in one night they had a wander through mine. Fortunately they desisted after 3 weeks, when rain storms made it easier for them to find worms and slugs in nearby fields.

On any bare soil for new sowings, neighbouring cats are often unwanted visitors. If they start to dig holes for their defecations, you need to lay bird netting over beds until plants are established.

Toad! Good for slug recycling.

Fleece is known as 'row cover' in the USA.

Soil pests

Raising plants on areas that were previously grass carries a particular risk of soil pests, and in temperate areas there are two significant ones, leatherjackets and wireworms. Check with local gardeners to see if they know of any others that cause problems.

Slugs

Often the most common soil pests in temperate climates are slugs (or snails, which are essentially slugs in shells), and they can do frightening amounts of damage, mostly at night. If you are sowing and planting close to walls, bushes and any damp and darker areas, expect some problems, especially in mild, damp weather.

Slugs are more common in the first months after clearing surface growth and weeds, so don't be discouraged if you suffer them at first. When you follow the tips below, their ravages will lessen; there are no magic bullets, but these methods help to avoid the worst.

- Habitat reduction: keep areas to be planted clear of vegetation, weeds included, for at least a month beforehand.
- Population reduction: either keep a 'lure' in place, such as a plank of wood, which then needs checking and slugs cutting or removing regularly; or venture out at dusk on a damp evening, with torch and knife – you may be surprised at the slimy carnival that awaits you.
- Risk reduction: sow and plant in season, so that seedlings have the most appropriate weather for the best chance of outgrowing some nibbling. See Chapters 9-11 for advice on timings as well as on sowing methods.
- Have at least one small wild area in your garden, where predators such as toads, slow-worms and hedgehogs may live; sometimes a compost heap is enough for this.

So many slugs after a wet autumn, on calabrese.

The third point above relates to slugs' useful role of recycling nutrients by speeding the decay of weak leaves and plant growth generally. Sowing at the right time gives more chance of having healthy plants, which are less interesting to slugs.

Leatherjackets

These soft but tough, unattractive larvae grow from the eggs of crane flies (daddy longlegs or harvestmen), usually laid into grass such as lawns. They are common after wet summers, when the eggs hatch more easily in damp soil from July to September, and in mild winters. Their larvae are brown and without an obvious head or tail, just a huge mouth (it seems!) eating roots and leaves close to soil level.

Throughout my first spring at Homeacres I had many lettuce, spinach and beet plants suddenly keeling over, or massively eaten of their lowest leaves. Rummaging with fingers under affected plants often revealed a brown larva, then a week later there would be more damage and I would find another one. It was bearable, just, with most plants surviving, and although the losses look dramatic, subsequent growth tends to fill in the gaps. After planting it is worth hanging on to surplus plants for a while, so you can put them into any bare spaces that are created. Leatherjacket damage ceases in early summer when the larvae stop eating and pupate. Alliums, potatoes, legumes and most larger plants survive the root-grazing.

Wireworms

These are the larvae of click beetles, 3cm (1") long, white or pale brown in colour, more rare than leatherjackets but also more dramatic and difficult to do anything about. Fortunately they are unlikely to be a problem unless you are taking on an area of south-facing, long-term grassland. Most damage occurs after July, so growing early crops followed by a green manure of mustard will reduce damage to vegetables.

Other grubs

Woodlice become numerous in mild weather and where the soil contains woody debris. Although mostly keen to eat old wood, they do like the stems and leaf margins of spinach, tomato, cucumber and many other plants. Their grazing shows as serrated edges to leaves, and there is no remedy except to keep wood on the soil to a minimum.

Chafer grubs, fat and mostly white, are the larvae of flying beetles and sometimes eat the roots of vegetables and strawberries. However, they cause much less damage than leatherjackets.

Ants cause problems in summer by harming plant roots with their acid secretions, and by 'farming' aphids for their honeydew. Ants crave warmth and like the wooden sides of beds; watering them helps keep their numbers down. Biological controls exist, but it should be possible to live with ants.

CHAPTER FOUR

Clearing ground

Eliminating weeds and waste material

"Sweet flowers are slow and weeds make haste."

William Shakespeare: *Richard III*, Act 2, Scene 4

This chapter describes ways of clearing ground as quickly and as simply as possible. I have separated the process out into two distinct stages, to clarify what needs doing, according to what you are faced with. After the first stage of clearing, you can see more clearly what is needed for you to have soil ready for gardening. The complete removal of weeds may take months, but by using the methods described here, within a year you should have clean soil, for minimal effort.

Homeacres when I arrived, in November.

Stage 1: woody growth, stone and rubbish

The first stage is to clear excessive vegetation, especially plants with woody stems, so that you can see the weeds and other plants underneath. If there is a lot of tall growth, some surprises may await you at ground level, such as rocks, tree stumps and man-made rubbish.

Dealing with woody growth

If you are faced with woody vegetation, the first step is to clear both surface growth and roots of brambles, bushes and ivy. These may look daunting, but are often quicker to clear than masses of leafy weeds. I use a scythe for larger areas of brambles and tall, stemmy weeds, and a pair of secateurs with gloves for odd plants, but larger woody material needs a pruning saw or even chainsaw.

If you don't have a mechanical saw, it may be worth hiring one or paying someone to do the initial cutting of wood. In November I was fortunate to have the help of my friend Robin, a gardener, who produced an amazing machine from the boot of his car which looked like a cross between hedge trimmer and chainsaw. Two hours of cutting with that, while Steph and I cleared a mass of ivy, made an encouraging start.

Woody growth is all compostable, providing you have the time and tools to chop or shred it finely enough. Piles of brambles and twigs can be assembled for a rotary lawnmower to chop up or, if you have regular quantities of woody prunings, a shredder is worthwhile. Shredded prunings provide a good balance in compost heaps with green waste from the garden, and I

A big bonfire of conifer branches and leaves.

have seen lovely compost in my neighbour Gert's garden, although his shredder is noisy to operate.

I had too much to shred after the conifers were cut, and burned the leaves as they were felled. Then the next morning I shovelled up the glowing embers of charcoal before they turned to ash, for spreading on some of the new beds. Charcoal is good for long-term fertility, to hold nutrients at least, and is more valuable than wood ash, which is mainly calcium carbonate, and the main plant nutrient it contains is potassium, which is water soluble. So ash is best spread around growing crops, which will take it up quickly, rather than on unplanted ground, where it is at risk of leaching away in winter rain; or spread it under cover, where watering is controlled. Small amounts are good on a compost heap.

Removing roots that grow again

Many deciduous trees grow new stems from old trunks, and it is practical to use these every year as a source of poles for supporting plants or for firewood, but if you need to remove a large tree stump, call on a tree surgeon. Conifers do not re-grow, so I left the stumps of the old windbreak in place, as they were not in the way; their roots slowly rotting in the soil over several years and providing habitat for wildlife.

On the other hand, any smaller shrubs growing in places where you want to plant or make beds need the main crown of roots removing, to prevent regrowth. A combination of sharp spade and axe is enough to expose and then cut through the main roots and to prevent regrowth.

Brambles are nasty, thorny weeds, and you need to dig out their main

Left: I dug out these bramble and dock roots. Right: Surface roots of bindweed after being covered with light-excluding mulch.

roots only: look for the clumps of stems, and cut into the soil around them with a sharp spade, to remove about 15cm (6") of main root. All their fine roots can stay in the soil. Brambles that are cut only at soil level will keep re-shooting, so it really is worth digging out the main crowns.

Ivy is invasive, but has quite shallow roots that mostly come out when pulling on the above-ground stems. You will subsequently find ivy growing from seed, but it is easy to pull when small.

In the front garden, I was disappointed while pulling ivy to find many white, fleshy roots of hedge bindweed (*Calystegia sepium*). This weed is extremely persistent; however, after a year of either mulching or regular root removal with a trowel, it has almost disappeared from my garden. By comparison, field bindweed (*Convolvulus arvensis*), whose roots are smaller but deeper-growing, is still present a year later, slightly weaker after a year of weeding (see pages 62-3 and table on page 65).

Clearing stone and rubbish

In the initial clearing stage it is worth removing all surface debris of old bricks, concrete, wire, polythene and stones bigger than a tennis ball, to make subsequent work such as hoeing and sowing easier. You need to do this only once in order to benefit from an easier soil surface in years to come. With a no-dig approach you can leave any deeper rubble and rubbish undisturbed.

While digging holes for apple trees and a trench for the polytunnel cover, I found that the soil at Homeacres contains a fair amount of undesirable history: shards of glass, bits of rusty metal, wire, the odd fertilizer sack and also areas of gravel from old pathways. I would prefer that it was not there, but feel that it is better to leave it in place than to cause massive soil disruption by trying to remove it.

Stage 2: clearing weeds

This stage is key, and not only because weeds grow fast. They will easily grow to outnumber and outgrow new plantings, then drop large amounts of new seeds before dying, or, in the case of perennial weeds, endure for years with roots that multiply and spread. Most gardens have a large reservoir of weed seeds and roots, although until the soil warms up sufficiently for them to spring into life, it is hard to know what will grow. Be prepared!

Be ambitious

Aim to clean your soil of almost all weeds in year one. The 'almost' is because bindweed and marestail will linger (see below). Apart from them, you *can* have clean soil, and the extra time needed for this in year one is repaid many times thereafter. An important part of this process is to clean the soil in pathways too, unless you have wooden-sided beds with mown grass around them. See Chapter 6 for more on making beds.

After the perennial weeds are gone (or almost gone), by year two, no light-excluding covers are then required, although some gardeners choose to continue using them. For growing most vegetables and flowers in clean soil, it is simplest to have just a surface layer of compost, which can be sown or planted into at any time, and means fewer slugs present than under mulch covers (see Chapter 5 for more on both approaches). Newly germinating weed seedlings are quick to keep in check with a little-and-often approach to weeding.

Different approaches for annual and perennial weeds

Existing annual weeds are simple to clear by mulching, as we saw in the example of my first project in Chapter 1, and illustrated in the photos overleaf (for more on mulching see Chapter 5). But the common difficulty is a large reservoir of seeds in the soil. Annual weeds drop a lot of seed because new plants are their main means of surviving, whereas perennial weeds tend to seed less because they survive by roots as well.

1, 2 & 3. Mulching soil with compost and soil, then cardboard and polythene on top. **4.** May: mulches removed, and most of the weeds are dead. **5.** June: plantings of squash, beans and Brussels sprouts. **6.** August: strong growth; the Brussels under fleece.

To clean soil of perennial weeds, in contrast, you must be consistent and thorough, using these two main approaches:

- Light exclusion with appropriate mulch materials, for as long as it takes.
- Using a trowel to remove the top growth of roots when you see any new leaves.

This process is explained in detail on pages 62-5.

A quick, easy approach for all new weed seedlings

Weed seeds germinate whenever they are exposed to light, from the soil surface being disturbed. A lovely aspect of no-dig gardening is that few weed seeds are brought up to the light and so the majority stay dormant. As a result, I spent remarkably little time on them in my first season, considering what a weedy mess Homeacres had been.

It helps to have a mulch of compost on top, even if it contains weed seeds of its own, because it has the advantage of being easier than soil to pull a hoe or rake through, or to scuff with a trowel, or to pull individual weeds out of.

When you have mulched with a layer of compost, be prepared in spring with a hoe, a rake or even just a trowel or any small hand tool, to scuff the surface as soon as you see the first signs of tiny green leaves. Do this when you see the first tiny shoots of weed growth, lightly and quickly. You'll probably need to do it every 2 weeks or so in early spring, when many seeds are germinating after changes in temperature and daylight length have broken their dormancy.

The smaller weed seedlings are, the more likely it is that gentle, shallow movement of surface soil and compost will kill them. You need only move the top 2cm (1"). In early spring this is quick, easy and saves immense amounts of time in the weeks ahead.

Hoes come in many shapes and sizes. See if you can borrow one, to find a blade and handle length that suit you. Then a hoe becomes your trusty friend, saving much time and effort for little use. The thin blade of an oscillating hoe is effective, and its side bar prevents the accidental cutting of plant roots.

A medium-to-narrow rake is a good tool for scuffing and moving the thin surface layer of beds and any exposed paths, lightly and horizontally, before weed seedlings can establish any root system. Small weed seedlings that you dislodge in any fashion are unlikely to re-grow, whereas larger ones might, because they have a greater store of food and take longer to shrivel. If possible, do your hoeing and raking on the morning of a bright and breezy day, so the weed roots dry quickly.

This method cleans soil and composts of the weed seeds that germinate after winter. Later in the year, a few seeds will germinate of different weeds, whose dormancy is broken by increased warmth and longer days: just keep looking, and always make the small amount of time needed to disturb or pull them when tiny. This is far more agreeable than the much larger job later, should you not do it now: a stitch in time saves nine – at least. Furthermore, it means that you have the pleasure of clean soil around your plants, and the advantage of fewer hiding places for slugs.

In the long term, adopting this method means you are always reducing the store of weed seeds that can germinate, because you are allowing none to seed. Your own compost becomes cleaner of weed seeds, and each year you need less time for weeding. It even becomes fun to weed when there are so few. Perhaps Robert Louis Stevenson was on to this when he said in 1890, "Nothing is so interesting as weeding. I went crazy over the outdoor work, and at last had to confine myself to the house, or literature must have gone by the board."

Perennial weeds

Perennial weeds have strong-growing roots and also often have a dormant period, staying invisible with no surface leaves for weeks or months. Bindweed is a good example, invisible for up to 6 months until its roots suddenly spring to life in spring warmth and then grow all summer.

Without mulching, perennial weeds are time consuming and difficult to eradicate (with the exceptions of brambles and stinging nettles). Whereas covering them with a light-excluding mulch, for sufficient time, starves roots of their food stores and sees them all die off.

The roots of perennial weeds are hard to dig out successfully because of two main attributes, which vary with different weeds:
- Their durability after being cut – they will grow again from small pieces, especially after rotovating.
- Their depth in the soil – sometimes out of reach and impossible to remove completely.

These factors make a mulching approach much quicker, with the potential to completely eliminate the weeds, as long as you follow up with a trowel on any surviving growth in the ensuing months (see page 64) – maybe for as little as 1 month for buttercup, 2 months for dandelion, 4 months for couch grass and a large, uncertain amount of time for bindweed.

At Homeacres I was faced with plenty of perennial weeds – all the ones in the table on page 65, except ground elder and marestail. But just 9 months after laying my first mulches, the only survivor was bindweed and a few weak roots of couch grass. The only one left after another 9 months is

Left: Many roots of couch grass in this soil (my greenhouse!).
Right: Couch grass re-growing beside a lettuce in April.

field bindweed. Eradication of the majority of persistent weeds makes gardening much simpler thereafter, and saves a lot of time.

Light exclusion

The aim is to prevent any light from reaching the successive new leaves of perennial weeds, whenever the soil is warm enough for them to attempt new growth. Then, because the new leaves cannot photosynthesize, food stores in the weed roots are not replenished and eventually they wither to nothing.

The table on page 65 gives a rough idea of how much time is needed of light deprivation for different weeds to die. There are no precise figures, of course, because it depends on how large and vigorous the weed roots are to start with, and also how warm the weather is: die-back happens more quickly in warm soil, as 'futile growth' is more rapid. By contrast, winter mulching of most perennial weeds has relatively less effect.

The table refers to total light exclusion, and does not apply to thin organic mulches, which allow some weed leaves to grow through. All the weeds shown in this table will send some new growth through a mulch of compost or other organic matter, and this regrowth needs removing every few days until the parent roots are exhausted. If you won't have time to do this, a light-excluding cover is the best option: see Chapter 5, page 71. The figures I give for time needed to exhaust roots are on the generous side, and you may succeed more quickly – it depends partly on how well established the weeds are. When using polythene covers (see page 76), a

1 & 2. June, and this mulch of landscape fabric was allowing many weeds to grow, especially bindweed.
3 & 4. So we replaced it with polythene, and by November most weeds had died from lack of light.

longer period of mulching is preferable to removing a mulch earlier and then having to deal with regrowth from surviving roots.

Using a trowel

The main point of no-dig gardening is to avoid inverting or even disturbing soil and its precious inhabitants. However, the occasional intervention of a trowel, using it as a lever but moving soil as little as possible, is helpful for extracting the top 7-15cm (3-6") of perennial weed roots, whenever you see new green leaves. In warm weather, this is best done little and often, once or even twice a week, so there are fewer leaves to send food back to the inaccessible, deeper roots. These therefore become weaker every time you weed, from their sending up shoots and receiving

Light exclusion of perennial weeds

Weed	Rooting habit & average depth	Dark-time to exhaust roots
Bramble (*Rubus fruticosus*)	Forking, woody; 10-45cm (4-18") Best to dig out root crown	Best to dig out root crown
Couch grass (*Agropyron repens*)	Tough, white spears; 5-15cm (2-6")	8-12 months; remove any new growth
Cow parsley (*Anthriscus sylvestris*)	Tap root, forking; 18-45cm (7-18")	8-12 months
Creeping buttercup (*Ranunculus repens*)	Spreading, tenacious; 7-10cm (3-4")	4-6 months
Creeping thistle (*Cirsium arvense*)	Brittle white roots; 15-30cm (6-12")	3-6 months; then pull any new shoots
Dandelion (*Taraxacum officinale*)	Tap root, thin; 15-25cm (6-10")	6-9 months
Dock (*Rumex obtusifolius*)	Tap root, sinewy; 20-30cm (8-12")	10 months; large roots best dug out
Field bindweed (*Convolvulus arvensis*)	Deep, twisting; 1-2m+ (3-6'6"+)	12-24 months; also needs continual removal of shoots, persists many years
Ground elder (*Aegopodium podagraria*)	White, shiny; 20-25cm (8-10")	10-12 months; remove survivors
Hedge bindweed (*Calystegia sepium*)	White, fleshy, brittle; 5-25cm+ (2-10"+)	8-12 months; remove survivors, is eradicable
Lesser celandine (*Ranunculus ficaria*)	Small, brittle bulbs; 5-7cm (2-3")	4-6 months from late winter
Marestail (*Equisetum hyemale*)	Wiry, tough, found in damp soil; probably up to 5m (16')	Years! Roots are resilient
Stinging nettle (*Urtica dioica*)	Yellow, thin, spreading; 5-10cm (2-4")	6-9 months or dig out

almost nothing back, so that new shoots become thinner and eventually (except for bindweed and marestail) cease altogether.

A good tool helps: I use a trowel made of 95 per cent copper, with 5 per cent tin for strength. Even in its fourth year of use for weed control, the blade stays sharp, thanks to the metal not rusting. This also keeps it smooth, and the trowel is thin enough to slip easily in and out of soil with little effort and causing minimal disturbance.

When mulching is thorough and weeds are cleared initially, subsequent weeding is quick and straightforward: stay vigilant for small weeds and deal with them as soon as you see them. This is helped by making beds with good ingredients and in such a way as to both reduce weeds and increase the growth of the plants you want – covered in the next two chapters.

CHAPTER FIVE

Mulching

An easy way to reduce weeds and improve fertility

"A weed is a plant that is not only in the wrong place, but intends to stay."

Sara Stein, author of *My Weeds: A Gardener's Botany*

Using a mulch to clean soil of weeds is an excellent way to save time and effort. Moreover, mulching with organic matter not only adds fertility but also allows you to grow plants while the weeds are dying. Choose which mulch to use according to how much time you have available, the climate and what type of weeds are growing. This chapter compares the benefits of organic matter and of light-excluding covers as mulches, and also discusses other ingredients that can be added to soil to improve its quality. In my garden at Homeacres I mulched extensively as a way of both clearing weeds and feeding the soil, and created an abundant garden very rapidly, as illustrated in the examples in this chapter.

Mulching: what, why and how?

A mulch is any material that can be spread or laid to cover the surface of the ground. Some mulches are thin and some are thick; some exclude all light and some do not; some are organic material and some are plastic. Examples include compost, cardboard, wood wastes and polythene of many kinds. Compost is a variable product, as its quality is affected by its ingredients and how they were handled. This is covered in detail in Chapter 6 (see pages 99-103).

There are many and varied reasons for using a mulch:
- to kill existing weeds by starving them of light, with minimum effort
- to reduce the growth of new weeds, saving much time
- to feed the soil (in the case of organic mulches), by feeding soil organisms as well as adding nutrients
- to preserve the existing soil structure and cause no damage to its inhabitants
- to protect the soil surface from wind, rain and sun
- to have a clean surface for walking on.

Whichever of these reasons is your priority will influence which mulch is best for you. For example, if you are faced with a large number of persistent perennial weeds (see Chapter 4 for more detail), black polythene is worthwhile. If you want to plant straight away on weedy ground, a thick mulch of compost is good. You can combine mulches too – for example by spreading organic matter before laying polythene, to feed soil life while killing weeds very effectively (and worms love the darkness under polythene).

Time saving

An important reason for mulching is to save time in the busy growing season. When I look at the large area I garden at Homeacres, I shudder at the thought of attempting to manage it by digging followed by hand-weeding and hoeing. High numbers of weeds usually appear in disturbed and bare soil, then in any damp weather they are difficult to remove from sticky soil, or to hoe.

Another way in which a soil-feeding mulch saves time and adds value is by increasing the yield from a given number of plants. For the same

1. February: clearing a path edge before mulching with cardboard. 2. Biodegradable polythene laid on the pasture.
3. The near half has compost on top of the polythene . . . 4. . . . while the back half has compost first, then polythene
on top. 5. June: growth was good on both halves. 6. September: second plantings of lettuce and radicchio.

amount of time spent planting and caring for plants, you harvest more produce as a result of increasing fertility.

Mulches of compost save waiting time too, because when the top layer is reasonably fine, you can sow or plant immediately if it is the right season. There is no need to wait for underlying weeds to die, because plants grow initially in the compost and then root more deeply into the soil below as it becomes available to them, with the dying weed roots leaving myriad networks of soil channels.

Another way in which mulching saves time in the growing season is that you can do it in winter: spread compost and/or cover ground with any other mulch you choose, in almost any weather during the winter half of the year. At Homeacres I started on waterlogged soil in December and had created most of my beds by the end of March – mostly in weather when soil cultivation would have been impossible.

How to mulch

The main considerations when deciding what approach to take are:
- how much organic matter to use for mulching, of what kind, and how well decomposed
- how long you will need to leave a light-excluding cover in place
- what you can grow in or through mulches while weeds are dying
- what characteristics of your garden may influence the suitability of different mulching materials.

Organic matter

The key factors in deciding what kind of organic matter to use are:
a) whether, in general, you have damp or dry conditions; b) your soil type.

In a dry climate or on sandy soil there are advantages in using organic materials in an undecomposed state, because these help to retain valuable soil moisture, as long as the mulch is not too thick or dense to prevent the passage of rain through it.

However, in damp climates, especially on heavy soils, this approach is disastrous, because it affords moist shelter to slugs and they breed underneath. In much of the UK, where the weather is generally damp, the best mulch is compost (any well-decomposed plant and animal residues), which serves as a nice-looking and warming addition to the topsoil, protecting the surface from sun and rain, and without providing habitat for slugs.

How long before compost is usable?

Different composting processes, ingredients and ambient temperatures mean that it's not possible to be precise about timing. Home-made compost is often ready to use after 8-10 months, but compost that is turned every week in summer may be ready within 1 or 2 months. Animal manures containing straw bedding are best when at least a year old, and for beddings of wood shavings you need 2 years or even longer. Leafmould takes 1-2 years to compost, but less time if the leaves were shredded and/or mixed with some manure.

How to tell when compost is usable

Compost is suitable for mulching when it is dark in colour, reasonably uniform yet often variable in appearance, more crumbly than lumpy, and with few unrotted ingredients visible. Composts that have been mechanically turned, and therefore become hot through the encouragement of bacteria, will look almost perfect but tend to lack important fungi, which have been killed by repeated turning and heating, whereas home-made compost may look uneven but is usually full of vitality.

You will help any lumpy and imperfect-looking compost to finish breaking down by spreading it on soil, exposing it to air and weather. Useful bacteria can multiply in the newly available oxygen and speed up decomposition – another reason for adding compost on the surface rather than digging it in.

It is sometimes advised to sieve compost before spreading on soil, but I never do, and find that it breaks up nicely over a few months. Any small pieces of twigs and fibrous material are not a problem, but I would pull out larger pieces of wood, and any plastic if you see it.

Light-excluding covers

There are many options to choose from with light-excluding ground covers. The materials are not always pretty, but they are only temporary, and using them makes time for other jobs. Over many years, including through the first year at Homeacres, I have compared the effectiveness of different materials to kill weeds, finding that they all have merits in different situations, and different drawbacks too. These are summarized in the table on page 73 and described in the following pages.

Slugs like living under dark covers, so I use this type of cover as a once-only method for killing weeds, for however long that takes. At

1 & 2. First spreading of soil and compost in March. **3.** Biodegradable polythene laid on top. **4.** May: watering newly planted squash; on the left are potatoes. **5.** June: potatoes and squash growing well. **6.** August harvest of 'Setanta' potatoes.

Homeacres, 4 months was the longest period for which I used polythene to cover ground, except on the front border, where hedge bindweed was deeply established and I was in no rush to plant, so I left it covered for a year. The bindweed is now almost gone, and I saved a huge amount of weeding time.

Light-excluding cover options

Cover	Qualities	Relative cost	Time to lay	Useful life	Drawbacks
Cardboard	Thick is best, not shiny card	Free but needs time to take off tape & staples	Moderately slow	2-4 months, useful in paths	Short life, fragile when wet
Carpet, used	Must be old, 100% wool carpet	Free if you can source it	Quick, though heavy	1 year or more	Rarely available
Landscape fabric, non-woven polypropylene	Black, lightweight, lets rain & some light through	Often a quarter of the price of woven fabrics	Quick but needs card beneath if many weeds	Rarely more than 1 year	Lets some weeds grow, breaks easily then messy
Landscape fabric, woven polypropylene	Black, lets rain & only 1% light through	The most expensive material	Quick	Often over 10 years	Expensive, shreds if cut, weeds can grow from above
Newspaper	Lightweight, may look messy	Free	Slow, takes time to overlap & secure	Up to 6 months	Time-consuming to lay, small pieces
Paper, sold as a mulch	Thinner than cardboard	Expensive relative to durability	Quick	1-3 months	Short life, easy to tear, costly
Polythene, black usually, non-bio-degradable	500 gauge or thicker*	Good value, can be found for free	Quick	Many years, goes brittle eventually	Does not allow water through, ultimately breaks, pollutes
Polythene, black & bio-degradable	Soft, fragile, transmits some light	Expensive because can only be used once	Quick but needs care not to damage	3-6 months but then decomposes slowly	Some weeds grow, 'litter' while degrading
Straw, hay or grass clippings	Permeable to some perennial weeds	Cheap if available as waste	Medium	6 months or more	Weed seeds, slugs
Wood shavings	Variable size, best on clean soil or over other mulch	Free if available as waste	Quick	3-9 months	Weeds can push through

*Gauge means thickness, e.g. 500 gauge is 125 microns (0.125mm) or 5/1000" thick.

Pros and cons of different covers

None of these materials offers all the answers for weed control, so take some time to consider their relative merits before committing to any purchase. Often it works well to combine different materials, such as cardboard or newspaper and wood shavings, and bear in mind that you may have minimal need of these cover mulches if your soil is already reasonably free of weeds.

Cardboard

Where there are many vigorous perennial weeds, I find that cardboard starts to rot before they are dead. When this happens, you need to put another layer of card on top of the previous layer (just leave the first in place). Some of my paths at Homeacres had three applications: in late winter, late spring and late summer. Although this approach takes more time than using plastics, there is no cost at all, and cardboard is eaten voraciously by worms when damp, so it never needs removing.

Carpet

Brandling worms (the sort you get in compost heaps) love wool carpet and help it to disintegrate within a year, especially when it stays damp. Light exclusion is good with carpet, for long enough to eliminate most weeds before it decomposes itself. Also, it lets rain through, so do use it if somebody gives you some; however, it does give shelter to slugs. Do not use carpets with synthetic components, as some of them may be harmful to soil life.

Landscape fabric (non-woven)

Landscape fabric transmits some light, so it works well in combination with organic matter or cardboard underneath. At Homeacres, before laying it, on some beds I spread 5cm (2") of compost or soil on the weeds; on other beds I spread a layer twice as thick and added some overlapped cardboard in a few areas too. Weed suppression in the case of the thicker layer of compost or soil was good, whereas buttercups, dandelions and couch grass grew through the 5cm mulch and then found enough light to continue growing under the fabric. These weeds were weakened, but it was still necessary to roll the fabric back and extract the new weed stems with a trowel, several times. The best weed suppression came from laying cardboard with the fabric on top – it also holds the cardboard in place, and looks nice. The photo on the right shows weed regrowth under fabric, and we put cardboard on them before re-covering with the fabric on top. When using this fabric, I suggest you use it as top layer and only for 1 year until it starts to decay: if covered with organic materials such as wood shavings or compost, it will gradually break up underneath them and out of sight, to create a messy layer of polypropylene in the soil.

Soft fruit bed: weeds growing under fabric, through 7cm (3") of compost.

Landscape fabric (woven)

Although expensive, this is a proven material, designed for the job. It is most worthwhile if you envisage several seasons of use, especially where you want to be rid of couch grass, bindweed and marestail. Beware of the messy shreds after cutting: to avoid this, either buy a roll or pieces of the size you need, or use a blowtorch to cut it and to burn planting holes with clean edges.

Paper or newspaper

In the first year of making my new garden, I bought an expensive proprietary paper mulch and found it almost useless for killing established weeds. It is better for use on clean soil, to prevent the growth of new weeds only. Newspaper is thicker and effective, but has so many edges to secure against wind that it needs many stones or wood, small lumps of wet compost, or piles of straw or hay along the edges and overlaps.

Polythene (non-biodegradable)

Polythene is good for reasons of ease and simplicity, and if you have a large sheet there are fewer edges to worry about (see opposite). I bought some cheaply from a farmer who was otherwise sending it for recycling, after he had used it for 11 years on a lambing polytunnel. It is green on one side and white on the other, and allows so little light through that all weed leaves quickly turned white, just as with 500-gauge black polythene. After 3½ months in spring, the buttercups were all gone, and most dandelions too. The couch grass was struggling although still there, but with occasional weeding after that, it had completely disappeared by the end of summer.

Polythene (biodegradable)

This stuff, made from corn starch, sounds like a great idea, but it is fraught with difficulties: for one thing, how biodegradable is it? Does it take 6 months, 6 years or 60 sixty years? Does it need light to biodegrade? I am not sure that anyone knows, but it soon tears into smaller pieces and the garden is then full of black scraps which look like plastic. The version I had (shown in the sequences on pages 69 and 72) was expensive and also too thin to mulch perennial and established weeds – bindweed grew happily underneath it and couch grass leaves pierced through it.

Straw, hay or grass clippings

These mulches add fertility in the long run and are useful for moisture retention in dry areas, but in damp climates they tend to harbour slugs. Also, they often contain weed seeds, which grow if the mulch wears thin, so you need to keep it topped up. Most annual weeds are effectively controlled, but some perennials grow through and need repeated pulling.

Wood shavings

These are of variable size, from sawdust to woodchips. A mid-range size of wood shavings is most useful as a path mulch, directly on soil, its thickness proportionate to the volume of weeds: if there are many, I would put cardboard down first. Wood shavings break down slowly enough to suppress weeds for several months and do not rob soil of nitrogen when used as a surface mulch. Eventually they turn into a black soil food of high quality. Avoid using any wood waste from treated timber whose chemicals risk contaminating soil.

Edges

Light and weeds creep a surprisingly long way under the sides of any cover, so all edges within a mulched area need overlapping by 15cm (6"), to ensure complete darkness. Perennial weeds are the most spreading.

Pushing the mulch edge into the soil.

You need to lay weights along the outer edges of a mulched bed or plot, so that grass and weeds cannot push it upwards and cause light to enter from the side. I use stones every 45cm (18"), or lengths of heavy timber and fence posts – whatever comes to hand. Alternatively, if using fabric or polythene, you can push its outer edges into the soil, which is what I did for the long, thin beds with newly planted fruit trees. Use a blunt spade, so the mulch material does not tear as you push it into the soil. This prevents grass and perennial weeds from spreading into the compost of beds' sides, and means one less job to do in the growing season, when maintenance of edges can be time consuming.

Choosing the right mulch for the situation

From the wide range of options you need to choose the most suitable mulch for your plot, bearing in mind the time available before you want to plant, and the materials you have to hand. Every situation is different and every plot has different weeds.

For example, if taking over an allotment full of perennial weeds, I would cover with polythene or Mypex for a half or even whole year before attempting to grow plants. You could probably crop while mulching like this, through holes (see the example on pages 79-80), and regularly remove any perennial weeds that popped out of those same holes.

If perennial weeds are not too vigorous, and you want to plant straight away, a mulch of up to 15cm (6") of any compost is good, so long as it's reasonably fine in the top 5cm (2"), for sowing and planting into. However, it is vital that you continue weeding any new growth with a trowel, until the

October harvest of squash 'Crown Prince' and 'Buttercup'.

weed roots are exhausted. On the whole, if a lot of perennial weeds are present, a light-excluding cover is worthwhile, although you lose time waiting for weeds to die.

The advantages of compost mulches are:

- You can sow and plant as soon as plants are ready and the season is right.
- The surface is open to air, resulting in fewer slugs.
- Compost improves fertility in both the short and the long term.
- The thick layer is necessary once only to clear weeds; in following years 3cm (1") is enough to mulch and feed.
- It looks great.

If you don't have access to enough compost for a thick layer but only enough, say, for a covering of 3cm (1") or less, then you also need to use one or more of the various light-excluding covers on top, for the length of time as recommended in the table in Chapter 4, page 65, depending on what weeds are growing. For the least time needed for laying, ordinary polythene is efficient and cost-effective. Woven fabric, such as Mypex, is more expensive but is equally quick and allows rain through. If you have more time, cardboard works well, but be careful to overlap its edges and re-cover with another layer before weeds grow through.

Other soil additives

Soil can be encouraged to grow healthier plants by the addition of other ingredients, such as rockdust, seaweed or charcoal, mostly for the purpose of adding trace elements (see box on page 81), or, in the case of charcoal,

Potatoes with black polythene and cardboard

It is possible to grow some vegetables while using light-excluding mulches to kill weeds. Large plants, which need few holes, are the most suitable; for example courgettes, squash, cucumbers and potatoes.

I grew 'Estima' second early potatoes where a pile of manure had sat from October to February, killing most grass but leaving many roots and shoots of couch grass, cow parsley and field bindweed. On top of the undisturbed and firm, rather weedy soil I spread 7cm (3") of composted cow manure and then laid some old black polythene to prevent weeds re-growing, and to keep light off potato tubers as they developed in early summer.

We planted through holes in the polythene in early spring, using a trowel to set potatoes into the soil surface, just under the compost. After 3 weeks their shoots appeared through the small holes in the polythene, some needing help to find their way out.

By early summer there was abundant growth. We had dry weather, which was ideal, with the polythene retaining moisture and most of the rain trickling gently into the planting holes. The summer harvest of 27 plants gave 27kg (60lb) of waxy potatoes. Gathering them was easy because the tubers were not deep in soil. I simply cut off the top growth for composting, rolled back the polythene cover, and pulled the stems of each plant, to reveal clean yellow potatoes nestled

Site of manure heap for 5 months; some weeds remain.

April: planting potatoes through black polythene.

June: card over holes in plastic to keep potatoes white.

Under the polythene, an 'Estima' potato plant.

20kg (44lb) of potatoes from this area, nestled in compost.

in compost, sometimes with a few slugs underneath.

I was lucky that the dry spring had reduced slug activity: this can be a problem with growing potatoes under mulch. In this case there was a good harvest and the couch grass was nearly gone, while the bindweed was much weakened.

This bed was quick to replant, on the same day as the potatoes were harvested: I used a trowel to extract the remaining weeds, walked on the surface to break up lumps and to level the compost, then dibbed holes for purple sprouting broccoli and calabrese, which I had been growing in modules for a month, and watered them in.

for holding on to nutrients. They can all be spread on the surface in small quantities, or raked in.

Rockdust – fine waste from basalt quarries

There is no hard proof of, or consensus on, the value of rockdust to plant growth, but there is plenty of favourable anecdotal evidence. Sometimes rockdust acts like a magic key to unlock hidden potential in soil, and its greatest benefits have been shown on soils where plants were still struggling after other efforts to improve growth had proved ineffective. Also, best results are found when the dust is literally dust for the most part, rather than tiny pieces of rock.

Trials I have done show small increases in growth and quality of plants, but then my soil was already growing healthy plants before using rockdust.

Rockdust should increase the amount of trace elements in soil over a long period, as it decomposes slowly, and its ingredients become more available to plants after being eaten by worms, which appreciate its slight grittiness for their gizzards. Look for fine dust without too much small gravel. If you can buy more cheaply in bulk bags of a ton, perhaps sharing some with friends, it is well worth using.

The usual recommendation is to spread a handful every square metre (10 square feet), though good results have come from using less. Using more may be beneficial, but increases the cost. I add a little rockdust to all my potting composts.

Trace elements

Sometimes called 'minerals' or 'micronutrients', these are a very small percentage of most soils' ingredients. Even in such tiny amounts, they are chemicals needed by plants for healthy growth. Examples of trace elements that are necessary for the health of plants, animals and humans but are occasionally deficient are manganese, selenium, iodine and boron, while sometimes they can be poisonous to life, as with lead and mercury. The additives mentioned here, except charcoal, contain a wide spectrum of health-giving trace elements.

Seaweed

There is no doubting the value of seaweed and its wide spectrum of trace elements; the question is availability. If you are near the coast, I would recommend fetching as much as you can or are allowed, for spreading in autumn and winter as a 5-7cm (2-3") mulch, except where sowing small seeds in spring. Vegetables that originated by the sea, such as asparagus, seakale and the brassica and beet families, show the most benefit, often with significantly improved growth. If you don't have access to fresh seaweed, dried seaweed is an option. It is easier to spread but more expensive.

Charcoal

The use of charcoal in farming and horticulture is a much-debated topic, but I have had some disappointing results here in a trial comparing it with other soil amendments such as compost and rockdust (detailed overleaf). Its claimed attributes are to hold on to nutrients, lock carbon into soil, help soil organisms work better and hold extra moisture. However, it does not contribute nutrients of its own, and in my trial, the soil containing a proprietary charcoal, 'GroChar', which has small additions of worm casts and mycorrhizal fungi, grew the lowest yield of tomatoes and potatoes.

Soil additives experiment: GroChar, compost, trace elements

I ran the following trial to assess the effects of different soil additives, by comparing the growth of tomato and potato plants.

In April we filled three sacks of 33x45cm (13x18"), normally used for growing potatoes, with a clay-based topsoil and different additions, mixed into the soil before filling:

1   A bucket of 1-year-old home-made compost, making 30 per cent by volume of the total growing medium.
2   4.5kg (10lb) of GroChar 'soil improver' (a proprietary mix of charcoal, mycorrhizal fungi, worm casts and seaweed), making 10 per cent by volume, as per instructions on the packet.
3   One cup each of dried seaweed, rockdust, volcanic lava and wood ash.

First planting

I planted 'Sungold' tomatoes on 2 May, one in each bag, and one sweet basil plant also. The sacks were placed against a south-facing wall and it was a sunny spring and summer, so by mid July I picked a truss of 20 tomatoes weighing 90g (3oz) from bag 1. However, there was no first truss on the plants in bags 2 and 3.

By early August all three bags were cropping well, still with slightly more

Steph fetching soil for the trial bags.

Left to right: seaweed/minerals, GroChar, compost.

'Sungold' tomatoes in August, with basil too.

tomatoes on bag 1, and I stopped the plants by pinching out their growing points, with five trusses to come on bag 1, and four trusses on bags 2 and 3.

By 5 September fruiting had finished, with all tomatoes ripe except for three on bag 2. I had not recorded weights because of the irregular harvests, but I measured the diameter of the plants' main stems at 1m (3') high, and weighed the bottom 1m of stem from each sack when removing plants in early September. The results are shown in the table below.

October: after the tomatoes, 'Charlotte' potatoes.

Second and third plantings

Then in each sack I planted a 1-year-old tuber of 'Charlotte' potato, grown through summer on a windowsill, where they slowly sprouted until I planted them in pots in mid August, to start growing while the tomatoes were finishing. They grew fast after being planted in the three bags, and I harvested them on 14 October, after blight in early October had killed most leaves, though there was less blight on the plant in bag 2.

Next I spread 2-3cm (1") of home-made compost on bag 1, two handfuls of GroChar on bag 2 and 1cm (½") of rockdust on bag 3, before planting three 'Grenoble Red' lettuce in each bag. They gave leaves for 6 months, until starting to make a stem the following May. The quality was good throughout this period, thanks to a glass window panel leaned over the bags from November to early April.

The photos show the differences in the appearance of the plants in the three bags, which reinforces the figures in the table, indicating that compost-grown vegetables crop well and are healthy, rockdust shows promise, and proprietary charcoal composts are perhaps more for long-term benefit rather than for feeding soil in the shorter term.

Soil additives experiment			
Bag	Tomato stem width, early autumn	Potato harvest, mid autumn	Lettuce harvest, winter & spring
1 Compost	2.2cm (7/8")	310g (11oz)	600g (1lb 5oz)
2 Charcoal 'soil improver'	1.6cm (5/8")	250g (9oz)	610g (1lb 6oz)
3 Seaweed & minerals	1.5cm (9/16")	160g (6oz)	700g (1lb 9oz)

CHAPTER SIX

Building beds

Experimental results from beds with different ingredients

"There are no gardening mistakes, only experiments."

Janet Kilburn-Phillips, English cottage gardener in Cincinnati

One quick way to start growing vegetables or other plants is to put a wooden framework on the ground – however weedy, stony or whatever it may be – and fill it with compost or good soil. In so doing you can transform a weedy mess into a surface for sowing and planting into, within a few hours. This chapter describes my experiments at Homeacres with variations on this approach – comparing growth in, for example, beds filled with different ingredients on top of undisturbed soil. Paths and edges are important too, so you also need to consider whether to build your beds with sides or without, and how to mulch your paths.

Creating beds – wooden-sided or open-sided?

If you make beds without any sides on weedy ground, there is a 'no man's land' of shallower compost at the bed edges, as it tapers down to path level, where the weeds aren't effectively mulched. This can allow perennial weeds to survive, allowing those such as couch grass and dandelions to shoot upwards along the edges. Weeds need to be mulched with the same thickness of compost right to the bed edges, so any kind of side to a bed is useful, in the first year at least.

Frameworks of wood make it much easier to create new beds, to establish their shape, to mulch weeds up to the edges and to keep the bed contents separate from path mulches. However, in the longer run there are potential drawbacks, as the wood decays and provides a home for slugs, woodlice and ants, maybe other pests too. To avoid these issues and to save the time and cost of making permanent wooden frameworks, you can shape beds with temporary borders of wood, just sitting on the surface if the wood is thick (say 7.5cm/3"), or thinner wood can be held in place with stones, both of which methods I used for the new beds at Homeacres.

October: this temporary wooden side also served as a slug trap.

December: the last stage – wooden sides removed, and wood-shavings manure on paths.

Wooden sides in year one

When making my new beds, I used wood from the old post-and-rail fence as temporary sides, simply laid on the soil. They not only kept a higher level of compost in the beds' sides but also prevented it from falling on the mulch of cardboard in the pathways, which ensured that the path mulches were more effective, with the cardboard staying drier and impervious to weeds. To sum up this most important point:

- The wooden posts or rails sit on the cardboard's edge and keep shape along the beds' sides, ensuring an even depth of compost right up to the edges, until the compost settles and becomes firmer after a few months.
- Wooden sides keep compost off the paths' cardboard, making its mulching more effective. This applies equally to other path mulches, such as woodchip and wood shavings: in fact, if you like clean, wood-mulched paths, it is probably worth having wooden sides to your beds.

After year one

At the end of the first year, when the main bulk of perennial weeds is gone, you can remove the wood from bed edges. The exceptions are where you have just one or a few beds in amenity areas, or have mown grass paths, or for school projects, for example, where wooden sides make a clear definition to the growing area.

Beds with no wooden sides worked well here, but there were no perennial weeds.

Pests associated with wooden bed sides

At Homeacres I left just a few beds wooden-sided, where I wanted definition for specific experiments. Elsewhere, every time I lifted wood to remove it, I found slugs and their eggs, of all sizes, shapes and colours. They love the humid darkness of wood where it makes contact with soil, using it as a base both for night-time foraging of leaves, roots and fruits, and for breeding. So:

- If slugs are a problem for you, keep wooden bed sides to a minimum, apart from when you are starting out and need to contain a sufficient depth of compost to smother perennial weeds.
- Furthermore, use an occasional plank lying on soil as a slug trap, remembering to lift it every morning if possible, to remove or cut any sheltering molluscs.

In addition to the slugs, there are often many woodlice living under wood and foraging outwards from the home it affords. Woodlice like to eat leaves and stems of spinach, beetroot, tomatoes, beans and cucumbers, and the roots of celeriac. They are especially active in the drier conditions of greenhouses and poly-tunnels, so keep wood to a minimum in protected areas, where woodlice appreciate rotting wood and the dry life, and multiply quickly. They increase as wood decays, indeed they help it to decay, so the problems of old wooden sides are likely to outweigh any advantages.

Different path mulches: cardboard, compost and part-rotted manure.

Keeping paths clean

The difference between years one and two is most apparent in pathways. Gardening is easier when paths are clean, with no weeds spreading into beds, by either dropping seeds (annuals) or spreading roots (perennials). At Homeacres, the presence of many perennial weeds, such as couch grass, meant that diligent mulching of paths was needed for most of the first growing season, until the weed roots were exhausted. Halfway through the first autumn, the paths were clean of new growth from perennial weeds – all that remained were dormant roots of bindweed.

Once paths are mainly clear of perennial weeds, you can spread a light dressing of any partly rotted organic matter, such as woody municipal compost, wood shavings or strawy material (if slugs are not a problem), to achieve a clean and easily maintained surface. For extra fertility, and especially when beds have no sides, a 5cm (2") layer of compost on clean paths is a good investment, making them easier to hoe and weed, while vegetables and flowers in the beds will send roots outwards to use that fertility and moisture.

Remaining weed roots, of bindweed and marestail for example, will send new growth upwards in the following growing season, and this needs occasional but regular removal to weaken the roots (see Chapter 4, page 64).

Filling the beds

How much compost and other organic matter you can make or get to your growing site will influence which of the methods you choose for building your beds. Soil without the addition of garden compost or manure is an option, when fresh and full of life. All the examples described in the rest of this chapter, in which I experimented with different materials for filling my beds, or in some cases just as a surface layer on the existing pasture, are about two things happening at the same time: mulching weeds and growing food.

Using a cardboard mulch on beds

Cardboard is a convenient mulching material, and can be used on or within beds to reduce weed growth. However, mostly there seems little benefit to be gained from using cardboard as a bottom layer in beds, because under the bed filling it softens quickly and soon allows weeds to push through it. This happened in two beds I made in late April, whose first layer was cardboard on pasture, with 10cm (4") of compost on top. Within 4 weeks, there was plenty of couch grass and bindweed pushing through, and I needed to use a trowel frequently after that.

The other side to this is that a cardboard layer that stays dry and

Left: Bed made in April, with cardboard below compost.
Right: In July there is couch grass pushing through.

prevents weeds pushing upwards may also prevent plant roots passing downwards. In any long spell of dry weather, if using this method I suggest watering plants thoroughly enough that any new, unrotted cardboard below them is moist. Also, if the compost layer on top is 5cm (2") or less, use a dibber or trowel to make a hole in the cardboard just below any plants you are setting out.

By contrast, in a nearby bed I had created 2 months earlier, with just 5cm of compost but with some thick cardboard on top held down by stones, there was less eventual perennial weed growth than in the more thickly mulched bed with cardboard underneath. This shows how cardboard for weed suppression is most effective on the surface, kept uncovered as much as possible – just with whatever it takes to weigh it down, particularly along any edges next to strongly growing weeds and grass.

In a similar vein, I experimented with a proprietary paper mulch (see Chapter 5, page 75), both under compost and on the surface, and was unimpressed by its flimsiness – certainly no good against perennial weeds. It is much thinner than cardboard and is expensive too.

To clear vigorous perennial weeds, you can use cardboard underneath beds in drier situations, such as a greenhouse or polytunnel, where you have the ability to control moisture levels and the cardboard stays dry enough to serve as an effective weed barrier. In my greenhouse, where couch grass was well established, I laid thick sheets from removal boxes on the weeds, then 20cm (8") of compost on top. I did not water for the first 2 months, when most beds were empty, and saw almost no couch grass at all, just some bindweed by late summer. However, when plants are growing larger in such beds, again you need to be sure to water enough that the cardboard moistens and allows their roots through to moisture below. You can check on moisture levels by using a trowel or dibber to see what is happening at depth.

Beds on undug pasture, filled with either soil or compost

Made: December, 2 beds of 1.2x2.4m (4x8').
Depth of ingredients: 15-20cm (6-8").
Similarities: Some growth and harvests of vegetables were better on one bed; some on the other. The final result was broadly the same.
Differences:
- The surface level of the compost bed shrank, while that of the soil stayed constant – awkward for annual topping with compost.
- The bed with soil had more weeds; the bed with compost had glossier leaf growth.

Preparing the beds

In this experiment I filled two wooden-sided beds with a good depth of soil or compost, on top of grass and weeds. I used healthy topsoil from a nearby part of the garden, where a concreted area, perhaps the base of an old shed, had acquired soil on top and was growing abundant stinging nettles and grass. Nettles are a sign of healthy soil. So I cleared them to the compost heap, together with their larger roots, and moved the soil directly to fill the bed. It needed about three-quarters of a ton of soil to fill its frame.

The soil-filled bed shares an end with another wooden frame of the same size, which I filled with the ingredients of a 2-year-old bed from my previous garden at Lower Farm, which contained a mix of old composted manure and garden compost. It was black and crumbly, and I finished the bed with 5cm (2") of 1-year-old compost on top.

The compost needed extra firming in order to fill it with a similar weight of growing medium to the other bed, because it is less dense than soil. The weight of material used was similar, but the compost bed's surface was slightly above the wooden sides after filling, then it sank during the following year to a similar level as the soil bed.

1. December: wooden frames laid on pasture. 2. The first bed being filled with compost. 3. The further bed being filled with soil. 4. Still December: first planting of perennial kale. 5. May: growth is similar on both beds.
6. June: healthy potatoes, garlic and broad beans on the compost bed.

Results

I expected the compost bed to grow larger and healthier vegetables than the bed of soil. In fact the differences were small, as shown in the table opposite, and some vegetables, such as early potatoes, garlic and hearting cabbages, grew larger in the soil bed, whereas beetroot and endive were more productive and had glossier leaves on the compost bed. See page 99 and also Chapter 8, page 130, for comments on this result.

The total yield of vegetables until December was 20kg (44lb 1oz) from the compost bed and 19.1kg (42lb 2oz) from the soil bed.

Left: June harvest of 'Swift' potatoes in soil bed, 1.4kg (3lb 1oz) from one plant.
Right: The beds in July – compost bed on left; soil bed on right.

Left: July still – with beetroot planted a month earlier beside shallots; red flax too.
Right: December, before spreading compost on top. Kale keeps growing.

Beds on undug pasture, filled with soil or compost				
Vegetable*	Planted	Harvested	Bed with higher yield	Comments
Kale 'Taunton Deane' (perennial)	Dec	Apr–Dec	Compost	Prolific on both beds
Broad bean 'Aquadulce'	Dec	Jul	Soil	Similar harvests
Garlic	Dec	Jul	Soil	Lovely bulbs
Shallot 'Red Sun'	Mar	Jun	Soil	Shallots on soil all bigger
Potato 'Swift'	Mar	Jun	Soil	Stronger plants on soil bed
Onion sets 'Stuttgarter'	Apr	Jul	Compost	Bulbs on compost bigger (opposite of shallots)
Beetroot 'Boltardy'	Jun	Aug–Dec	Compost	Large roots over a long period of harvest
Cabbage 'Christmas Drumhead'	Jul	Oct–Dec	Soil	Firmer hearts on the soil bed, two only on each
Kale 'Redbor'	Jul	Oct–Dec	Compost	One plant on each bed, both good
Endive 'Aery'	Sep	Nov	Compost	Brighter green on compost bed

*Listed in order of planting date.

Weeds

The main difference between the beds was the thick quantity of new weeds germinating on the soil bed, while there were few on the compost bed. The soil weeds were difficult to hoe because they were growing in damp clay, and on three occasions two of us spent a whole hour pulling speedwell, grass, celandines, buttercups and bittercress out of sticky soil. "Tickle the earth with a hoe, it will laugh a harvest" (Mary Cantell) – but you can hoe only when soil is reasonably dry, and it rarely was. The soil did laugh a harvest in the end.

By late spring the surface of the soil bed was clean and drier, and it was easy to hoe lightly. This soil is not being dug, so no more weed seeds will be exposed to light, and subsequent years will see far fewer new weeds. I spread compost on the surface of both beds at the year's end, so the experiment is now diluted, but the beds may yet show interesting differences.*

*In the following year (2014), growth was noticeably stronger on the compost bed.

Beds on undug pasture, with or without composted manure on top

Made: February, 2 beds of 2x9m (6'6"x30'); both initially mulched with 800-gauge polythene.
Depth of ingredients: Nothing added to the soil bed, 5cm (2") composted manure to the compost bed.
Similarities: Only in the growth of beetroot.
Differences:
- Earlier growth of vegetables and larger harvests on the bed with compost on top.
- Slightly fewer weeds on the bed with compost on top.

Preparing the beds

This experiment came about as a result of a suggestion of a course student in March, to whom I was explaining an existing experiment to compare growth in dug and undug beds, neither of which had any compost added (see Chapter 8). She said, "Why not add a third bed, undug and with compost added on top?"

We created a bed of the same size as the beds in the related experiment (described in Chapter 8) by spreading a thin layer (5cm/2") of 2-year-old cow and horse manure on top of pasture – containing grass, buttercups and dandelions. The soil-only bed was simply an area of pasture of the same size, with a 45cm (18") path between the two beds. Steph helped to cover both beds and the path with one large sheet of polythene, at dusk

Left: In April, spreading compost before re-covering with polythene. Right: In May, after removing mulches: the soil-only bed has a surface of yellow, dead grass.

on a cold winter evening. This light-excluding mulch over its weeds was the only treatment the soil-only bed had.

I removed the cover in mid May and found that 11 weeks in darkness had been enough for the grass and buttercups to die, while dandelions were still making some new, yellow leaves. It took 20 minutes to trowel them out, and all was ready for the first plantings.

Results

In this experiment there were differences between the two beds, both in total yields, as shown in the table below, and in the timing of growth.

Yields from undug beds, first year from pasture; one with compost on top					
Vegetable*	Soil-only bed		Bed with compost on top		Comments
	kg	lb/oz	kg	lb/oz	
Beans 'Czar'**	0.83	1lb 13oz	0.75	1lb 10oz	Slow to establish on bed with soil only
Beans, borlotti**	0.23	8oz	0.77	1lb 11oz	Like Czar, slow starting
Winter squash 'Kabocha'	2.74 (2 fruits)	6lb 1oz	7.75 (3 fruits)	17lb 1oz	Slow to establish on bed with soil only
Winter squash 'Uchiki Kuri'	3.07 (4 fruits)	6lb 12oz	8.95 (9 fruits)	19lb 12oz	Slow to establish on bed with soil only
Celeriac 'Prinz'	1.14	2lb 8oz	2.82	6lb 3oz	Poor roots, wood-louse holes
Beetroot 'Boltardy'	20.86	46lb	25.96	57lb 3oz	Late bulking on bed with soil only
Leek 'Zermatt'	1.37	3lb	2.48	5lb 7oz	Leeks like rich soil!
Leek 'Bandit'	3.36	7lb 7oz	5.55	12lb 4oz	Steady growth in winter after leek moth damage
Cabbage 'Filderkraut'	6.18	13lb 10oz	6.16	13lb 9oz	Impressive hearts, but damage from caterpillars
Cabbage 'Kalibos'	0.85	1lb 14oz	1.14	2lb 8oz	Low-yielding variety, caterpillar damage
Totals	40.63	89lb 9oz	62.33	137lb 4oz	

*Listed in order of planting date.
**Yield shown is of dried beans.

Both beds in early July: the soil-only bed on the left; composted bed on the right.

Planting into the soil-only bed was difficult because there was still a mass of dead and dying pasture roots, and the soil was still wet and sticky. Plants on this bed were slow to get going in early summer, which explains the huge difference in the yield of squash, whose main growth was finished by mid August. There were 12 squash from the two plants on the bed with compost on top, and 6 squash from the two plants on the soil-only bed.

Other vegetables continued growing through autumn and on the soil-only bed some almost caught up, growing extra fast from late summer, after the slow start. Cabbages on both beds had been massacred by caterpillars of various white butterflies and moths, throughout July and early August, until I sprayed their leaves with an organic spray, *Bacillus thuringiensis* ('Bt') – a soil bacterium that paralyzes the gut of caterpillars only. This needs repeating every 3 weeks, which I did at intervals of about 20 days. Subsequent growth was rapid and clean, but the loss of growth time in July meant that the hearts were not solid. 'Filderkraut', used for sauerkraut in Germany, has a sweet flavour and pointed hearts. I made some fermented *kimchi* from it, adding cucumber, onion and carrot: it is a powerful pickle.

The leeks were much damaged by moths laying eggs on to their heart leaves in early August, after which the caterpillars ate new, inner leaves until early October. This did not kill any plants but stopped them growing for a long period, and although regrowth of damaged leeks is rapid in the remaining warmth of autumn, from plants' well-developed roots, yields are cut by 50 per cent or more. In the bed with compost, plants both grew and recovered well. The compost also seemed to make a huge difference to the celeriac, confirming that they are hungry for the extra nutrients and moisture afforded by an addition of compost: a thicker layer would have been productive for them.

Conclusions

It was clearly worthwhile adding the layer of composted manure, into which plants could root while old roots in the soil below were still decomposing. Fibrous material, such as plant roots, contains a high proportion of carbon, which uses up nitrogen (also needed by growing plants) while it is decaying. Plant growth is slower for as long as this takes, then speeds up when it is finished and the decayed material, with its assimilated nitrogen, becomes plant food itself. In the soil-only bed, the absence of any added ingredients made it harder and slower for plants to establish into the dense soil where breakdown of the dense fibres was happening, of weedy pasture roots which had been alive and growing so recently.

By contrast, in the soil-filled bed of the earlier experiment (pages 92-5), the plants were able to root easily into the deep layer of good topsoil on top, and there was no 'nitrogen robbery' caused by decaying weed roots.

Beds on undug pasture, filled with garden compost or composted manure

In this and the next experiment I compared growth in beds filled with organic matter of different origin, without recording harvest weights – just watching growth throughout the season. There were fewer differences than I expected. The main difference was evident where I filled a bed with compost containing many woody fragments, and early growth was poor until midsummer, owing to nitrogen robbery by the wood while it finished decomposing.

Made: December, 2 beds of 1.5x5m (5x16').
Depth of ingredients: 15cm (6").
Similarities: In growth of weeds and most vegetables.
Differences: Slightly better growth of carrots and parsnips in garden compost.

Left: February – manure on grass on the left; compost on the right; paths mulched with cardboard.
Right: By June, early plantings are growing well of tall peas, beetroot, squash and onion.

Preparing the beds

I made the two beds in late December, simply by spreading home-made compost on the pasture to make one bed, and the same depth of 18-month-old cow manure on pasture to make the other bed.

Because these beds carried on from the main dig/no-dig ones (see Chapter 7), I lined them up in parallel and with the same 60cm (2') width of pathway, which was so that visitors could comfortably walk between the beds when looking at their differences or similarities. However, this width of path does mean a large area to mulch for no particular benefit. I needed to lay new cardboard three times on the paths – in January, May and August – to keep smothering couch grass, which finally disappeared by September. The couch grass kept re-growing through the beds' mulch and needed much trowelling of its new leaves and shoots. In the early stages of mulching pasture which contains perennial weeds that are vigorous enough to reach the surface through a mulch, and with a thick mat of roots below the mulch layer, all you can extract with a trowel is new shoots rather than existing roots.

Results

The growth of most vegetables, including onions, beetroot, broad beans, tall peas and tomatoes, was similar in both beds. But carrots and parsnips germinated and grew rather better in the compost bed, I think mainly because the compost was a little more decomposed than the manure.

Beds on undug pasture, filled with municipal (green waste) compost, soil with composted manure, and composted manure

Made: February, 3 beds of 1.2x2.4m (4x8').
Depth of ingredients: 15cm (6").
Similarities: Equal growth in the two manured beds, autumn growth equivalent on all three beds.
Differences:

- Fewer weeds on the bed with municipal compost.
- Stronger growth on manured beds until July, then more equal.
- Fewer slugs on autumn endives on the bed with municipal compost.

Preparing the beds

The three beds were made in a straight line, using a wooden frame, which was filled and the contents firmed with a spade. Then we lifted the frame off the bed with a person on either side, and placed it on the pasture alongside to fill the next bed. The frame ended up as an enclosure of the municipal compost bed, as I did not need it again that spring, so this bed was the only one of the three that had sides. In spite of this difference, there were slightly fewer slugs on this bed with wooden sides.

February: municipal compost at the near end; composted manure at the far end.

The first bed was filled with 18-month-old well-decomposed cow manure; the second bed half-filled with Homeacres soil, then the same 18-month-old cow manure on top; the final bed was filled entirely with municipal compost, bought as '15mm (⅝")' sieved', meaning it contained less wood and plastic than if had not been sieved. However, there was still a lot of wood in it, all in small pieces!

Left: Weaker onions on the bed of municipal compost; beetroot planted.
Right: Viewed from the other end – a bigger onion harvest on the composted manure.

First planting: onions

In early April I planted four rows of onion sets along the length of each
bed. From the beginning of their growth, the onions on the two beds
containing composted manure grew more strongly and consistently, yielding more than twice the amount of the onions harvested from the municipal
compost bed, some of which had simply not appeared, and many of which
were small. The obvious reason for this was the high proportion of wood
in the compost mix, still rotting and therefore demanding nitrogen to
break down, thus depriving any nearby plants.

Second plantings: beetroot and salads

Then in late June I planted a row of multi-sown beetroot modules (average
four per clump) along one side of all three beds, between two onion rows,
and was amazed to see how they grew more strongly on the municipal

compost bed, yielding about a quarter more by September than those growing in the beds containing manure, although these also yielded good-sized roots. Clearly, once the wood has done most of its decaying, nitrogen that was previously needed for decomposition became available to plants.

As well as beetroot, I planted lettuce and endive in early August and observed two small differences, in addition to there being fewer weeds in the municipal compost:

- Slightly fewer slug holes on those growing in municipal compost.
- A higher yield of leaves from those growing in the manure.

One conclusion from this experiment is that it may be best to keep woody compost for surface use only, where it is more a mulch than a growing medium. However, it's possible that if you can buy municipal compost with added compost or 'digestate' from food waste, in which the nutrient status is richer, the extra nitrogen will help to meet the demands of decomposing wood.

October: similar growth on both composts, of salads planted in August.

CHAPTER SEVEN

Dig versus no-dig (with compost)

Comparing growth with different methods

"I don't think we'll ever know all there is to know about gardening, and I'm just glad there will always be some magic about it!"

Barbara Damrosch, gardener and writer in Maine

There are times when digging is useful, such as to bury weeds for having clean soil to plant in, and quickly. If soil is crumbly and clean after being turned over, you can rake it level, then sow and plant straight away. Usually digging is done in late autumn or early winter, to allow time for weather to break up the soil surface and make a finer surface for spring sowings.

You can also make undug beds rapidly, when you have access to sufficient compost, as described in Chapter 6. Compost-filled beds can be sown or planted straight away, when the surface layer of compost is reasonably fine.

In my previous garden, at Lower Farm, I ran an experiment for 6 years comparing growth of the same vegetables on dug and undug beds. The results slightly favoured a no-dig approach in terms of yield, with the dug beds – single-dug, with compost incorporated – producing 376kg (about 829lb) of veg in total; the undug beds 400kg (about 882lb). So the experiment showed no increase in harvest from the extra work of digging. However, more weeds germinated in the dug soil.

At Homeacres I created a new dig/no-dig experiment, using two beds filled with the same amount of composted cow manure, and this chapter describes the results. Meanwhile, I had been persuaded by a chance meeting with some Japanese farmers to try a similar comparative trial, but without any compost in either bed. That trial is discussed in Chapter 8.

Setting up the experiment

I made the two beds in early December, with a framework of oak sides resting on level ground. They measure 1.5x5m (5x16'), and the planks are 20-25cm (8-10") wide. This makes them deeper than the beds in my experiment at Lower Farm, where the beds were 15cm (6") deep. See the beginning of Chapter 12 for more on how I assembled them.

Digging or filling the beds

While digging the dug bed, I found the roots of perennial weeds: only a small amount of couch grass, but plenty of dandelions and buttercups. The soil is reasonably dark and crumbly, as my spit (the length of a spade) was above the subsoil of clay below, but in one part of the bed I encountered a lot of gravel, where there must have previously been a path.

Using a sharp copper spade, I cut squares in the pasture of 25cm (10") and around 20cm (8") deep. All sods and soil of the first line across went into a wheelbarrow, then were used to fill the last trench at the other end.

This aspect of digging raises a question about the system of crop rotation to avoid disease, because when digging after cropping, one is moving soil from an end where, for example, there might have been leeks, and putting it in a different place where you may plan to grow leeks again: different place in the bed, same soil. All the surface soil of the dug bed moves along 25cm every year, and there is potential for spreading diseases, such as white rot fungi, in the process.

Steph helped to fill the trenches with a barrowload of 2-year-old manure in each trench, 20cm deep, then I turned soil from the next 25cm line, upside down on to the compost, thus creating a second trench across the bed, and so on. Steph moved nearly a ton of well-rotted manure that day, and between us we spent 8 hours making the dug bed.

The undug bed, by contrast, simply needed filling with compost on top of the undisturbed pasture, and this took 3 hours.

1. Starting to dig the dug bed. **2 & 3.** After each trench was dug, it was filled with cow manure . . .
4. . . . then the soil turves were replaced upside down on top of it.

Paths

For easy access and clear visual separation, I left wide, 60cm (2') pathways between and around the two beds. Until February these paths were grass and weeds: if left to grow, this would have needed cutting, and perennial weeds such as couch grass would have been pushing into the beds, with the greenery harbouring slugs. Whereas weed-free paths, in this case with cardboard initially and a thin wood mulch, offer moisture and nutrients to plants in the beds, and are quick to maintain once clean of weeds.

The first step, in late winter, was covering the paths with cardboard, being careful to squeeze it against the wooden sides: it is always at the edges where weeds reappear. Over this cardboard I spread 5cm (2") of fine wood shavings, the waste from a local joinery.

During spring and summer there were perennial weed leaves popping out along different edges, and in May they started growing more generally, as the cardboard decomposed. This meant laying another layer on top, and finally in October I put down a third layer of cardboard with another 5cm of wood shavings, to reduce mud, with the soil underneath being fully wet by then. This wood covering spreads the weight of feet and wheelbarrow, and is food for worms and soil life as it decomposes, all helping to keep air in the path soil.

February: after laying cardboard I am spreading wood shavings on top.

Sowings and plantings

The same seeds and plants went into each bed, at the same time. Direct sowings were made of broad beans, carrots and parsnips. Every other vegetable was sown in modules or seed trays in the greenhouse, for setting out as small plants, to increase productivity and the length of the growing season.

Growth of different vegetables compared

The table of final yields below gives a good indication of the differences in growth, showing how some vegetables slightly preferred the dug soil, some the undug, and that overall the harvests were similar.

Yields from dug / undug beds with compost				
Vegetable*	Dug beds		Undug beds	
	kg	lb/oz	kg	lb/oz
Broad beans	5.60	12lb 6oz	5.01	11lb 1oz
Shallot	1.91	4lb 4oz	2.55	5lb 10oz
Potato 'Swift'	2.98	6lb 9oz	2.36	5lb 3oz
Coriander / dill	0.47	1lb	0.47	1lb
Spinach	1.20	2lb 10oz	2.41	5lb 5oz
Lettuce leaves	8.32	18lb 5oz	9.85	21lb 12oz
Onion 'Balaton'	4.38	9lb 11oz	5.55	12lb 3oz
Onion 'Red Baron'	4.02	8lb 14oz	4.69	10lb 6oz
Beetroot (first sowing)	2.97	6lb 9oz	3.57	7lb 14oz
Carrot	4.12	9lb 1oz	3.26	7lb 3oz
Cabbage 'Greyhound'	4.17	9lb 3oz	3.70	8lb 3oz
Parsnip	7.74	17lb 1oz	7.15	15lb 12oz
Leek	4.24	9lb 6oz	4.79	10lb 9oz
Cucumber	0	0	3.29	7lb 4oz
Swede	9.25	20lb 6oz	7.92	17lb 7oz
Beetroot (second sowing)	4.34	9lb 9oz	4.66	10lb 4oz
Kale	3.83	8lb 7oz	4.64	10lb 3oz
Celery	3.37	7lb 7oz	3.35	7lb 6oz
French beans	1.64	3lb 10oz	1.74	3lb 14oz
Fennel	0.82	1lb 13oz	0.92	2lb
Endive leaves	5.65	12lb 7oz	6.22	13lb 12oz
Totals	81.02	178lb 10oz	88.10	194lb 3oz

*Listed in order of planting date.

May: early growth is slow in a cold spring.

The yield totals in the table are from small numbers of plants, mostly in one 1.5m (5') row across each bed, so they may be distorted by pest interventions, such as the vole which ate through the dug bed's cucumber stem. Therefore these figures should be taken as indications only, and in general the results suggest that vegetables grow well from both approaches. The following is an account of my observations of each type of vegetable in the two beds: crops are listed in order of the date of their first harvests.

Spinach

Harvesting period: 9 May to 21 June
In all 7 years of running these experiments, spinach has been the vegetable showing most difference, rooting faster and more strongly in surface compost than in dug soil. Its leaves are larger, darker green and thicker, and plants crop for a week longer before rising to flower in late June. In this case there was continual leatherjacket damage to plants on both beds, which reduced yields, even after I replaced a few plants. Spinach is fast-growing and finishes earlier than many other spring-sown vegetables, so I often plant swede after it, as that needs to be in the ground before the end of June.

Lettuce leaves

Harvesting period: 13 May to 13 August
There was a 3-month season of harvests off the same lettuce plants, over 750g (1lb 10oz) weekly from mid May to mid July, off the 22 plants in each bed. The varieties were 'Freckles' cos, 'Diveria' red cos, 'Bijou' red Batavian,

By July, each bed has already yielded 33kg (72lb 12oz) of vegetables.

'Chartwell' green cos, 'Lettony' green Batavian and 'Appleby' green oak-leaf. Batavian lettuce has thick stems with plenty of crunch, while cos lettuce is more upright and easy to pick (using fingers to hold the leaf while pushing downwards with the thumb to detach it from the stem). Each succeeding harvest, of all lettuce varieties, is quicker and cleaner, as the leaves are held more clear of soil.

A quarter of the plants on both beds were eaten at root level by leather-jackets (see Chapter 3, page 53) so I replanted twice to fill the gaps, ending up with 22 out of 24 plants on each bed. I watered them weekly from June when it was dry, giving them a thorough soaking each time. The best varieties in the July heat were Lettony, Appleby and Bijou, especially on the undug bed, with the weekly harvest on 16 July being 0.71kg (1lb 9oz) dug, and 1.11kg (2lb 7oz) undug. As they rose to flower in summer I pulled them for compost, and they were succeeded by the interplanted leeks.

Coriander and dill

Harvesting period: 21 May to 21 June
Growth of these herbs was similar on both beds, during harvests over a month from mid May. In mid June they flowered, and after pulling them out I planted beetroot.

Potato

Harvesting period: 12-27 June
Potato plants of first early potato 'Swift' looked stronger on the dug bed

throughout, while the tubers in the compost of the undug bed were cleaner at harvest time. I planted seed potatoes 10cm (4") deep, and they did not need earthing up. With first earlies, this is because they often finish growing before there is time to grow many tubers to push up to the surface. As soon as I had harvested two of the five plants, I planted cucumber in the gap, on 18 June.

Cabbage

Harvesting period: 21-28 June
'Greyhound' is an early variety: from late-winter sowings it grows firm, sweet and pest-free hearts, before there are butterflies to lay eggs and make caterpillars. Hearts on the dug bed were a little larger than those on the undug bed, and I have noticed before that early cabbage likes dug soil, although I don't know why. After harvesting, I planted their space with kale, making an eventual 8 months' worth of brassicas in that soil.

Beetroot

Harvesting period for 1st sowing: 27-30 June
Harvesting period for 2nd sowing: 15 August to 13 November
I sow beetroot in modules in the greenhouse, four seeds in each, for planting in clumps. The swelling roots push one another apart, and you can twist out the larger ones to harvest over a period of weeks. As with spinach, both beds needed some replanting after leatherjacket damage, with yields slightly higher on the undug beds, and I have seen this almost every year so far. Beetroot also makes a great second crop when raised in modules, already a month old at planting time, and the summer planting, after shallots, had roots ready to harvest by late July, after just 5 weeks in the bed.

Carrot

Harvesting period: 4-22 July
Carrots grew more strongly on the dug bed, until I saw some leaves collapsing in late spring. Voles like making runs under dug soil, where there is a loose zone between the upturned soil and firm soil below. They stay below ground to avoid their main predator, raptor birds. However, I tried peanut butter in a mousetrap, hidden under nearby parsnip leaves,

and caught two. After this I saw no more damage, although the dug bed's cucumber plant had been eaten through by then.

Carrots were straighter and smoother in the dug soil, and yielded better, despite the voles. In other years they have grown well in undug soil, but the difference here was a greater depth of slightly less mature compost than I normally use.

Broad beans

Harvesting period: 5-11 July
The beans were sown at Christmas and took 5 months to flower; later than usual. Broad beans like a warm spring but they do not like a hot, dry summer, and they matured all at once, with slightly more beans on the dug bed, although to the eye the plants looked identical in size and growth. Straight after the final harvest, I cut them at surface level to leave any remaining nitrogen nodules in the soil, and planted dwarf French beans in mid July.

Shallot

Harvesting date: 7 July
'Red Sun' shallots, planted in early March, grew steadily until some of the stems started to fall over in early July. After pulling I left them in the sun so the tops could die back, before bunching them to hang up. As with the other alliums (onion and leek) in this trial, those from the undug bed were larger.

Onion

Harvesting date: 4 August
As with the beetroot, I sowed the onions in modules, six to eight seeds per module, to grow in clumps of four to six plants, as I find that germination is usually variable with onions. Sometimes you can have up to eight onions in a clump, slightly smaller in size – if you want larger onions, thin them to three or four in a clump at planting time. Growth was good, under fleece for the first month – and in spite of the cold spring, when onions normally make a lot of growth, the harvest was only a week late, thanks to a hot July. The harvest from both beds was superb, as a result of plenty of sunshine through late spring and summer.

Out of sixty or so 'Red Baron' bulbs on the two beds, only three went to seed, far fewer than with red onions grown from sets, which are notoriously difficult unless you plant them in mid spring rather than early spring (although packet instructions normally advises earlier planting of sets).

Cucumber

Harvesting period: 11 August to 13 October

Outdoor cucumbers can be sown direct in early June, or, as I did here, in mid May in the greenhouse, to have two good-sized plants after 4 weeks. It was warm enough by then for good growth, until a vole ate the dug bed's plant stem.

French beans

Harvesting period: 21 August to 4 October

These beans were well on by early July in their modules, and so I planted them on the same day as I harvested the last broad beans, watering them well, as the soil was so dry. They cropped steadily for 5 weeks, although I found that this variety, 'La Victoire', made tougher beans and for a shorter period than my normal 'Cupidon' or 'Castandel'. There was little difference in growth between the two beds.

September: all second plantings except the parsnips, and over 44kg (97lb) from each bed so far.

Endive

Harvesting period: 2 September to 29 November

This was planted mid August after onions and in exactly the same spaces, so each row had seven plants of 'Bubikopf' scarole endive and seven plants of 'Fine Maraichere' frisée endive. The first pick of outer leaves was 3 weeks after planting, with leaves a little thick and large for the salad bowl, but with every picking after that, at 10-day intervals, the leaves grew finer and smaller.

I harvest with all the stems as well as green leaf, to reduce hiding places for slugs, which like endive stems: sometimes you need to trim off the stems before eating, when they have slug holes. There was consistently a 10-per-cent higher harvest on the undug bed, with leaves looking more glossy.

Kale

Harvesting period: 20 September to 4 December

If you want large kale plants, sow in April or May. For smaller ones with a fair yield, sow early June and plant after a harvest of, in this case, cabbage – or it could be broad beans, potatoes, etc. I planted three 'Redbor' F1 and two 'Cavolo Nero' kale in each bed, and they survived the July onslaught of butterflies and caterpillars until a massive infestation in late August, when I sprayed with *Bacillus thuringiensis* (Bt) (see Chapter 6, page 98).

The Redbor was tall, vigorous and gave 12 times the weight of leaves compared to Cavolo Nero: the red (Redbor) plants are graceful and decorative, though need staking in wind, and often survive winter. The kale harvest was higher on the undug bed – interestingly, since it was the other way around for cabbage, and both are brassicas.

Leek

Harvesting period: 3 October to 4 December

I interplanted the early leeks between lettuce (see Chapter 12, page 191 for details). I also planted four 'Bandit' leeks after potato, but the need to dig in December meant that winter growth was curtailed and they were small at harvest. Varieties such as Bandit, Apollo and Husky can sometimes double in size during mild spells in late winter. Growth was a little faster on the undug bed, and although plants on both beds were damaged by leek moth, there was a fair harvest after trimming.

October harvests of leek, kale, celery and fennel.

Celery

Harvesting period: 10 October to 14 November

I sowed 'Tall Utah' green celery in late May and planted it out in July, after carrots. Growth was steady with weekly watering and not too much slug damage, and harvests through October were similar between the dug and undug beds. Sowing late and leaving the celery unharvested until mid autumn was a bit of a gamble, as sometimes there can be a frost in early October, and I kept an eye on the weather forecast.

Fennel

Harvesting period: 10 October to 15 November

Fennel 'Montebianco' was sown in modules on 4 July and planted out 3 weeks later, after beetroot. Although overshadowed by the tall red kale, the plants grew steadily and swelled into medium bulbs through October, which was fortunately frost-free. Bulbs were a little larger on the undug bed.

Swede

Harvesting period: 10 October to 4 December

Growth was steady all summer and autumn, and the large plants of 'Friese Gele' spread out widely from August, after the nearby lettuce finished. The average weight of each root at harvest, after trimming soil and leaves, was 1.5kg (3lb 5oz) on each bed, but I lost one plant to disease on the undug bed, resulting in a difference in total yield.

Parsnip

Harvesting period: 13 November to 2 December
Sowing conditions for small seeds – parsnip and carrot – on the undug
bed were not ideal, with the compost more lumpy than I like it normally.
Both grew well, however, with some forked and some straight roots. Due to
the incessant rain of mid autumn there was canker on the roots' shoulders,
and this was worse on the undug bed – the main reason for its lower yield.

Weeds and pests

Weed growth on the two beds was similar at first. On the dug bed there
were thistles, grass and buttercups from previously dormant seeds, now
triggered into germinating by light. On the undug bed were mostly grass,
clover and fat hen from seeds in the compost. Both beds had an equal
number of perennial weeds trying to re-grow: after 4 months of removing
these new shoots, the only survivor was a small amount of bindweed.

By autumn there were few weed seeds left in the surface compost of
the undug bed, which was easy to keep clean. The dug bed continued to
grow grass in particular, which thrived in the damp autumn weather until
they were turned in while digging.

There were only two differences between the two in terms of pests and
disease: the voles which briefly lived in the dug bed and ate some roots,
and some extra canker on parsnip roots in the undug bed.

Conclusions

Overall, the results show interesting variations in growth of different
vegetables, but more than anything there were plenty of similarities. The
main difference between the two methods is the time and effort needed to
dig (5 hours in this case), which gave no obvious benefit in this experiment.

Some of the differences shown between the two beds are because it
was the first year of cropping after pasture at Homeacres. Six years
earlier, at Lower Farm, I had observed how the first year after pasture
favoured growth in the undug bed, where plants had easier access to the
surface compost. On the dug bed, they had to root through decaying sods
of grass and weeds, below a loose 5-10cm (2-4") layer of soil at the surface.

The next chapter looks at results from a similar experiment, but without
any compost added to the soil. My general conclusions from the experiments in Chapters 6, 7 and 8 are given at the end of that chapter.

CHAPTER EIGHT

Dig versus no-dig (without compost)

Comparing methods using a 'natural' system

"Gardeners must dance with feedback, play with results, turn as they learn. Learning to think as a gardener is inseparable from the acts of gardening."

Michael P. Garofalo, *Pulling Onions*

This chapter describes an experiment that is a useful comparison with the experiment in Chapter 7, in which compost was used, and may be of interest if you do not have access to much compost. In this version, the dug bed was simply dug, with no compost added, and the undug bed was covered with polythene mulch, starting in winter so that weeds were gone by late spring.

Natural Agriculture

I set up the trial as an attempt to understand Shumei 'Natural Agriculture', which is a way of farming that eschews any additives to the natural system. It is as much a philosophy as an agricultural blueprint, and the following description is very much abbreviated. For gardening purposes, however, we can say that the tenets of this method are:

- No crop rotation.
- Save your own seed.
- No compost used.

I had met some Japanese gardeners who grow this way, and became interested in their work, also noticing their lack of emphasis on methods of soil preparation, and thought it could be interesting to compare dug and undug soil in this system. In this first year of my experiment there was only one planting in each row, rather than successive crops – and later than usual, because the undug bed was not ready until late May, by which time its grass and weeds had died under the mulch that had been laid over the pasture in late January.

May, after first plantings (the dug bed in front).

No crop rotation

The reason given for not using a system of rotation is that soil organisms become adapted to the plants that are growing, and are then ready to work with more of the same in following years. This understanding, whether true or not, embraces a more positive outlook on soil life than the understanding of rotation as a means to avoid build-ups of pests and disease on plants of the same family.

However, to work well it needs home-saved seed, because the seeds grown in a particular garden or farm are adapted to its specific soil and conditions. In my case I had no seeds from this soil of a new garden, only some bean seeds saved at my previous garden.

Saving seed

The seed-saving part of Natural Agriculture is a skill to learn. Many vegetables are biennial, so do not make seed available until the following summer. An exception is beans and peas: I grow borlotti beans and 'Czar' runner beans, both of which you can harvest dry in early autumn, for eating in winter or whenever, and therefore you have seed automatically.

Squash too are easy to save seed from, but only when you grow just one variety (and no courgettes nearby), ensuring no cross-pollination by insects travelling from flowers of a related but different plant. This would create an unknown new variety the following year, which you may not like.

For true pollination of non-hybrid squash or courgette, you need to put a paper bag over the yet-to-open flower of one fruit (therefore female) in early summer, then, when it is opening inside the bag, pick a male flower on its stalk (male flowers have no fruit) and rub the two together to transfer male pollen on to the baby squash's flower. Re-cover the flower for a couple of days until it is wilting, and mark the fruit so you can identify it to save the right seed.

The previous year's harvests of runner and borlotti beans, used for seed.

For each other vegetable the seed-saving procedure is different, so it is worth reading up on the subject (see Resources). Saving your own seed will give you great growth, from fresher, often healthier seeds than those you can buy, but it needs attention to detail and, for certain vegetables, a fair amount of extra space in which to grow seeding plants.

Using no compost

This is the bit I find most difficult. In fact I notice some uncertainty in Shumei practice about whether to use any compost, but the official line is that soil has everything it needs when its organisms are working well. I am sure that there are also special cases of run-down soil where compost is allowed . . .

Setting up the experiment

On a freezing day in January, two visiting Japanese gardeners, Hiro and Ken, turned over the 2x9m (6'6"x29'6") area of pasture that was to be the dug bed. The soil was sticky but looked to have a good crumb structure, and developed a fine tilth in subsequent frosts. Through April and May I removed small amounts of regrowth of dandelion and buttercup, and hoed some annual weeds.

January: Hiro and Ken digging one bed, removing tree roots.

Mulch on the undug bed (on right).

Meanwhile the undug area, as well as the 45cm (18") path between the two beds, was covered with a large sheet of polythene to exclude all light. When we removed it in mid May, I was pleased to find most weeds dead, except for dandelions with pale, thin leaves. We used trowels to extract as much root as possible, which was difficult because the soil was firm and full of old pasture as well as some tree roots, from the spruce trees I had recently had cut down.

And that was it: ready to plant, no compost to spread (although I had put some on a third bed next to the undug bed, as described in Chapter 6 (see page 96).

Plantings and growth

Spring finally arrived, and the first plantings, on 22 May, were of both types of climbing bean, winter squash and celeriac, all sown earlier in the greenhouse. Planting was difficult in the undug bed, where the soil was sticky and felt dense as I dibbed or trowelled holes, compared with easier planting in the loose soil of the dug bed. After planting I laid a large piece of fleece over the whole area, because it was still cool at night, and windy too. There were slugs prowling around the bean plants, which were weak because of the low temperatures, and after a week I needed to replace 8 of the 24; some on each bed.

On the undug soil's surface there was a dense mat of roots, and I was worried that the polythene cover may have been on for too short a time, so that some of these roots might re-grow. And indeed, a fortnight after removing the cover, I saw green shoots appearing of grass and clover. Meanwhile, the remaining modules of vegetables were ready for planting, and on 1 June I planted beetroot, leeks and cabbages, laying cardboard between the rows on the undug bed to smother the attempted regrowth of pasture.

May: holes for beans in sticky, recently covered (undug) soil.

Planting was in lines across each bed, at the same spacings and done on the same day, so that there were no differences except in soil preparation. I watered very little through the dry summer, as the soil is heavy: it helped to have some heat in July to dry out the undug soil, and I think that in a wet climate where no compost is available, an initial dig of heavy soil may be worthwhile for this reason at least.

Early June: the beds now filled with recent plantings; the undug one has some cardboard mulch.

Weeds, slugs and a slow start on the undug bed

After a few days the cardboard was curling up along its edges, letting in light for weeds to re-grow, so I decided to remove it and skim off the surface 3cm (1"), turning it upside down as a mulch. Unfortunately this made the undug bed look like a dug bed, and then it developed a mosaic pattern as the turves dried and shrank – but it was effective for weed control.

Since the summer turned out to be dry and hot, in fact I could have left the pasture surface in place, and its remaining roots of clover and grass would then have shrivelled in situ. Whereas in a wet summer, the turf-flipping would have saved the day, so it was an insurance. Around the cabbages I left the turf in place, just to see, and all was well weed-wise.

Through the middle of June I needed to replace some slug-eaten cabbages, mostly on the undug bed. I had kept a few cabbages growing in small pots – it is a good idea to grow a few extra plants to keep in reserve.

Growth was steady on both beds except for wind-blown beans, and the undug bed's squash and bean plants were smaller and paler. I think this was from nitrogen robbery by decaying pasture roots (see Chapter 6, page 99), at a time when beans and squash want to grow fast and are hungry. On the dug bed, these roots had been decaying more quickly in the presence of extra air introduced by digging. This was less of a problem to the other vegetables on the undug bed, as they were growing more slowly at that time.

End of June: faster growth of squash and beans on the dug bed (in front).

Caterpillars on the cabbages

In early July I laid fleece over the cabbages, as there were sudden flocks of white butterflies, and through the subsequent hot weather there was a plague of them. Normally I cover with mesh because it is more ventilated than fleece, but I did not have a large enough piece for this cabbage area.

However, the fleece had a hole, and I never imagined the possible extent of damage that might result. Three weeks later I removed the fleece, after finding that caterpillars had been having a feast, safe from predators under the cover. The damage was far worse than on some uncovered brassicas, demonstrating the amount of caterpillar-eating that is done by birds and wasps.

Next I sprayed with Bt (see page 98), repeating every 3 weeks, which ensured clean hearts by October, although they were less dense than normal because of the time lost. The red cabbages never made up for a lost July and gave only small hearts, of an exquisite pink colour.

Left: August, with cabbages laced by caterpillars. Right: By October the white cabbages had recovered.

Harvesting and results

The table overleaf shows the final yields for each vegetable. See also the table in Chapter 6 (page 97), for a comparison between the undug bed shown here and an undug bed with compost on top.

Harvests started in September, with some large beetroot and all the 'Uchiki Kuri' squash, whose stems were dry already. They were of fine quality, with fewer and smaller ones on the undug bed, while the 'Kabocha' squash were ready a fortnight later, showing a similar difference between the two beds.

I then sowed white mustard (*Sinapis alba*) on the squash area, since it was otherwise to be bare soil for the next 8 months; this type of mustard grows 1m (3') high and is killed by moderate frost, leaving a strawy residue on the surface, into which I can plant squash again after some weeding on the undug bed, and digging the dug bed.

The bean pods were drying by late September, and I harvested them

September: the squash ready to harvest, and growth differences are evening out.

through October, with an earlier and larger pick on the dug bed. Yet the bean plants on undug soil, especially the 'Czar' runner beans, had almost caught up in late summer, after the slow start which reduced their ultimate yield. I made a final pick on 22 October, by which time there were few leaves on the plants.

'Zermatt' is a variety of leek for early harvest, and the plants had been struggling with damage from leek moth caterpillars through late August and September, when they otherwise grow strongly. Although they recovered after the caterpillars pupated in October, the overall harvest was

Yields from dug/undug beds, first year from pasture; no compost added					
Vegetable*	Dug bed		Undug bed		Comments
	kg	lb/oz	kg	lb/oz	
Beans 'Czar'**	0.95	2lb 2oz	0.83	1lb 13oz	Undug Czar grew well from August
Beans, borlotti**	0.57	1lb 4oz	0.23	8oz	Dug borlotti were always ahead
Winter squash 'Kabocha'	4.39 (3 fruits)	9lb 11oz	2.74 (2 fruits)	6lb 1oz	Faster early growth on dug bed
Winter squash 'Uchiki Kuri'	5.42 (7 fruits)	11lb 15oz	3.07 (4 fruits)	6lb 12oz	Faster early growth on dug bed
Celeriac 'Prinz'	1.51	3lb 5oz	1.14	2lb 8oz	Both beds showed need for compost
Beetroot 'Boltardy'	16.56	36lb 8oz	20.86	46lb	Beetroot likes growing in undug soil
Leek 'Zermatt'	1.60	3lb 8oz	1.37	3lb	Small growth, lack of compost
Leek 'Bandit'	3.03	6lb 11oz	3.36	7lb 7oz	Undug better yield after growing well through winter
Cabbage 'Filderkraut'	5.50	12lb 2oz	6.18	13lb 10oz	Strong autumn growth on undug
Cabbage 'Kalibos'	1.51	3lb 5oz	0.85	1lb 14oz	Dug good; undug suffered early problems
Totals	**41.04**	**90lb 7oz**	**40.63**	**89lb 9oz**	

*Listed in order of planting date.
**Yield shown is of dried beans.

disappointing. By contrast, 'Bandit' leeks are hardier and grow strongly through mild winters and into early spring, so I harvested them after the spring equinox, by which time the yield was higher on the undug bed.

Celeriac roots were small on both beds, which emphasized the value of adding compost for such a hungry and moisture-demanding vegetable.

Beetroot was the exception to most of the problems encountered by other vegetables: they simply grew and grew all summer and made some large roots, up to 1.5kg (3lb 5oz), even in the clumps of four together. Their late growth on the undug bed, with healthier leaves in October than on the dug bed, saw them finish with an exceptional yield.

Damage from pests was similar on both beds through the growing season, and by autumn, a look at the two together revealed far more similarities than differences.

Conclusions

The results suggest that when adding no compost at all, there are some benefits from an initial dig of weedy, grassy soil, for summer vegetables especially. Digging speeds the breakdown of organic matter, so that its nutrients are more available to plants. The digging was a day's hard work for my visitors, for a small increase in the total result and for faster access to soil for sowing and planting. On the other hand, if the pasture had been mulched since the previous autumn, there may have been less difference between the two, in view of how growth on the undug bed caught up from late summer onwards.

Growth on both beds was less vigorous than on the adjacent undug bed with compost added (see Chapter 6, table of yields on page 97), and growing vegetables without adding compost would barely be viable if starting with poor or compacted soil. The results achieved here were from a healthy and moisture-retentive soil of clay loam.

The main difference between the two methods in this experiment without compost is in the initial killing of weeds, which takes longer with mulching than with digging, but is much less work and is sometimes more effective. For example, if you were starting with a mass of perennial weeds such as couch grass and bindweed, digging will not kill them, whereas at least 6 months under polythene would be a good first step, entailing no digging at all (see Chapters 4 and 5).

Conclusions from the experiments in Chapters 6, 7 and 8

There were many variations in growth in the different beds in these experiments, according to whether soil was dug or not, how much compost was used, and of which type. Also, and in particular towards the end of this one growing season, there were many similarities too, showing that there is a broad spectrum of workable options for cleaning soil and filling beds.

Is it necessary to dig soil?

Yes if you have no compost for mulching the surface, and want to sow and plant immediately. Be prepared to spend a fair time digging, do a thorough job, and, if there are many perennial weeds, you will need time to remove subsequent regrowth with a trowel.

If you have enough compost to smother weeds, and only a small number of perennial weeds, it is quicker and easier to cover the undisturbed surface with compost, for less time needed and a bonus of bigger harvests from the enriched, undug soil. See Chapter 4, page 59, for more on this, and especially on the difference between mulching annual and perennial weeds. If you are not sure exactly what weeds and weed roots are present, I would use a light-excluding cover for 4 months initially (see Chapter 5, page 71). Then lift it to see if any new, white leaves are still growing in the darkness: if so, it needs to stay on, until only bare soil or compost is visible.

February: the bed on the left recently dug; leeks for later harvest.

For growing vegetables, is it necessary to add compost and/or soil?

Vegetables are hungry plants, and the results of the second experiment in Chapter 6 showed higher yields where compost is used. The first experiment in that chapter also showed good harvests from filling a bed with topsoil only, though there are two caveats to be made in that case: first, that it was high-quality topsoil, freshly moved and therefore still full of soil life; second, that in the following year the vegetables were generally smaller on the soil bed than on the compost bed, even though I spread the same amount of compost on the surface of both beds.

As noted in Chapter 5, a benefit of adding compost or soil to the surface, when there is enough to smother weeds, is that you can sow and plant straight away. Using a light-excluding cover as a mulch to kill weeds is effective, but entails a wait of around 3 months, often more where there are perennial weeds, before any planting is possible.

If your soil is reasonably dark and in good condition to start with, it is possible to grow without compost, but any amounts you can add, even small quantities, repay the effort.

Which type of compost is best?

The results in Chapter 6 show how caution is needed in filling beds with compost containing too much wood, but woody compost is effective as a thinner surface mulch. If free or cheap, using it as a mulch to kill weeds is viable – just be prepared for slower growth initially. Composted animal manures mostly contain more nutrients than composted plant material, depending on their age and the bedding used, but home-made compost is as good as any.

I cannot give any precise verdict about different composts, because they all vary so much – according to their mix of ingredients, the conditions of composting and their age. The nutrient value of compost is only part of the story, because all composts also increase moisture retention, and improve soil structure through an invigoration of soil life such as earthworms. I have often observed healthier growth from using compost, without plants necessarily growing much larger; they just have a healthy bloom. This caught my eye the most when using some worm compost (worm casts), although well-made garden compost comes close to that, because its final stage of decomposition sees the multiplication of worms, which eat and improve it. When using compost full of worms, or at the stage where they have moved on and left a soft, light humus, you need only half the amount, compared with less mature compost, for excellent growth.

PART TWO

Sowing and growing

CHAPTER NINE

Raising plants under cover

Methods and best timings, for earlier and better harvests

"I'm not ageing, I just need re-potting."

Anon.

There are many advantages to sowing plants under cover rather than directly in the ground outside. They grow earlier, more evenly and out of the way of pests. From this steady start, a greater reliability of harvests, over a longer period, repays the investment in materials and in any extra time spent. At least half of the vegetables you can grow in a temperate climate can be propagated in this way, for planting out in their final positions. Which you choose will depend on which are your favourites: in my garden, around 90 per cent of seeds start life in a protected environment, and this chapter explains how to do so for best results. The section at the end describes some vegetables which grow better from direct sowing, with tips on getting them started.

Benefits of raising plants under cover

The merits of starting plants under cover vary according to your climate, pest levels and how you like to garden. Most of the advantages come where the growing season is short, where spring weather is cool and windy, where slugs and birds are a problem, and when you want to increase the size of harvests over the whole season.

In such conditions, these are some of the potential gains:

- You can ensure a successful harvest from plants that would have barely enough time to mature if they were sown direct, such as winter squash and celeriac.
- You can add a month or more to the cropping life of plants that need heat to get going, such as tomato and sweet pepper.
- You get reliable and healthy plants from the warmer, calmer, drier and mostly pest-free environment under cover, ensuring full rows and beds outdoors.
- Many spring vegetables, sown earlier than is possible from direct sowing, give welcome food in the 'hungry gap' of spring.
- Spring-sown vegetables finish earlier, allowing more time to grow a second vegetable in the same soil during the remainder of a season.
- The harvests of second-cropping plants are greater, thanks to their 3-4 extra weeks' head start in modules, while the preceding crop in the space outside was finishing.
- Early sowing gives more time for harvests of plants whose flowering is governed by day length and therefore fixed; for example, spinach can crop twice as much from a sowing under cover in early March than from direct sowing a month later.

Module-raised lettuce and brassica salads.

Where to make early sowings

Outdoors in winter is too cool for almost any seeds to germinate, except broad beans and garlic in milder areas, so extra warmth and shelter is good. Options include a hot bed (see page 141, and also Chapter 14 for more about hot beds), while the cheapest structure is a cold frame – which you can also place on a hot bed.

Windowsills

Windowsills are useful for an initial fortnight at least, to help seeds germinate. Use them for this short-term boost to get seeds under way rather than for growing to planting-out stage, because seedlings cannot live too long in the one-sided light of windows before they become tall and thin – an exception being conservatories with light from more than one side and/or the roof. A drawback of this arrangement is that it may make a mess, especially when watering.

Garden structures

Any garden structure will be cooler than a domestic house by night and on dull days in winter, so germination is slower at that time. However, the all-around light means darker green leaves and sturdier stems than with plants raised on a windowsill. See Chapter 13 for more about large garden structures for under-cover growing.

Polytunnels are a little cooler than greenhouses, and with more potential slug damage from the damp soil along their edges. Just one slug or snail can quickly destroy many seedlings, so before sowing you need to check under any objects on the ground and under staging. Cold frames can host slugs and need extra attention: keep the area outside a cold frame as clear and open as possible, and go on a hunt at the first sign of damage. Keep a mousetrap on the go when sowing peas or sweetcorn.

Starting off your seeds

When seeds are fresh enough, and experiencing the right temperature for germination, they will grow for sure. There are many different composts and containers you can use, and sowing in warmth under cover is fun, because you can keep a close eye on progress.

The first seeds I sowed after arriving at Homeacres were peas (for eating as shoots), in January, in a module tray on a windowsill. They germinated well with only two waterings (it's a damp house), and I planted them in the polytunnel when a month old.

Immediately after the greenhouse went up, on 11 February, I sowed lettuce in trays and other vegetables in modules.

Late winter is a great time to start sowing and growing under cover, with the sun giving noticeably more light. Any extra heat you can provide enables plants to make more use of the improving light levels: at Homeacres, I made a hot bed (see page 142) inside the greenhouse.

April: peas, onions, beetroot and salads.

Compost for plant raising

You need a nutrient-rich material that drains well, yet also holds moisture. Peat does both of these things but is out of favour for environmental reasons, while garden soil is too dilute in nutrients, and often too dense as well.

I have had excellent germination and growth with both composted cow manure (18-month-old, contained straw bedding) and home-made compost. The bits of straw in manure and ligneous fragments in garden compost allow excess moisture to drain away, yet the compost stays moist and has a plentiful, slow-release supply of nutrients.

Buying compost for plant raising saves the time required for making your own, including the need to sieve it or chop and break the lumps. However, proprietary composts are of variable quality, so do your research, online or in magazine articles, to check on results of comparative trials (*Which? Gardening* does an in-depth compost trial each year). I buy organic multipurpose compost for most of my plant raising, from West Riding Organics, made with peat sieved out of reservoirs (as opposed to extracted from peat habitats).

Trays and pots

Trays need to be of firm plastic. Seed trays have no partitions, while module trays have individual cells, whose width and depth determine the size to which plants can grow in them: most vegetables transplant well from a width and depth of 3-4cm (1½"). Some, such as courgettes and tomatoes, need moving from modules into pots in order to keep them growing to a fair size before planting out.

Module-grown chard, ready to plant.

For most vegetables I suggest trays the size of A4 paper, with either 40 or 60 modules in each, to grow plants that are quite small and easy to set in the ground. With this approach you appreciate the efficiency of space that propagating plants affords; while providing warmth speeds the process, so you can also propagate more in a given length of time.

Pricking out

Often it works well to sow seeds direct into modules, but a few vegetables, those with tiny seeds or slow and uneven germination, can easily be sown in trays of compost, to prick out as seedlings into modules. Make sure the compost is moist, and use a pencil under their roots to lift clumps of seedlings. Then pull each one – by leaf or leaves, never the stem – and bury it into a pencil-sized hole in each module. Roots can be coiled in, there is no need to make them vertical. Vegetables I sow and then prick out are brassicas, lettuce, parsley, tomato, celery, celeriac, pepper, chilli and aubergine – the last five because they germinate so slowly, and lots of seeds can more easily be kept warm in a seed tray than in many pots or modules.

Tip: Bury stems when potting on. Every time you transplant or pot on any vegetable, bury the stem up to the lowest green leaf when possible, in order to make sturdier plants. Often plants can send new roots from the buried stem too.

Troubleshooting – when seeds don't come up!

Two likely reasons for non-emergence are that seed is too old, or it's too cold. In the first case, seed packets do not help, as they say 'packeted year ending . . .' rather than 'grown in year . . .' So they may be old when packeted, and I suspect that many are, especially from my comparisons between germination rates of packet seed and my own, fresh seed. When seedlings do grow from old seed, they are often weak and variable in quality. You could try different seed suppliers, and inform yourself about seed saving (see Chapter 8, page 121).

Warmth is a key factor, so refer to pages 144-5, and read up about each vegetable's needs in the next two chapters. Other possibilities are that you have not waited long enough (for instance, celery takes over 2 weeks to germinate) or that the compost is too wet, so don't water until it looks a little dry on top.

Watering

Watering is a skill to learn through careful observation, to ensure neither under- or over-watering. Compost in trays should often look a little dry on the surface, but never be so dry that it has shrunk and opened cracks around the edges. Water in the morning, so that leaves and all surfaces are dry by nightfall and less attractive to slugs. Watch the weather fore-cast, and water before all sunny days, maybe not at all before dull and cooler days.

Giving warmth to seeds and seedlings

It is amazing to observe how seeds germinate more quickly and seedlings grow more evenly when given extra warmth. You can buy kits of a thermo-stat and electric cable, to warm a bed of sand with trays and pots on top. It also works well to use indoor sources of warmth, such as cupboards with a boiler, to speed germination – just be vigilant and bring seed trays into light as soon as the first shoots appear.

The best time to apply warmth

Extra heat is expensive in time and money terms, and is most efficiently used in the first stages of growth. In particular, germination is like a hump in the way of eventual growth: once helped through it, plants can grow exponentially, because each new root and leaf is able to fuel more growth, in a virtuous circle.

Hot beds

Any 24-hour heat source ensures steady germination, which is otherwise slowed by cold nights in particular. One way of supplying heat, without any cost in electricity, is to make a hot bed, which is essentially a container filled with fresh manure (see Chapter 14 for more details). This gives off heat as it decomposes, benefiting seeds and plants placed on top of it. Horse manure gives off the most heat, but all manures can be used, and also any green wastes. The main thing is having enough to assemble an entire heap of fresh ingredients, to ensure the longest supply of heat. At Homeacres I am off-grid in the greenhouse, so made a hot bed inside it, using a neighbour's fresh horse manure (see overleaf).

You can make hot beds of different sizes and depths: when smaller and/or shallower, the temperatures will be lower. For example, you could put one underneath a cold frame, 30-45cm (12-18") deep, with seed and module trays on a wooden trellis sitting on the manure.

Warmth profile

Hot beds warm quickly, and after only 24 hours I have recorded 50°C (122°F) at 30cm (12") depth. In larger heaps, this core temperature can be maintained for at least 4 weeks, ensuring good germination and growth in trays on the pallet above, as its warmth drifts gently upwards. Sowings can therefore be made earlier, and in a mild spring, a hot bed filled in early-to-late winter can give enough heat for a 3-month season of plant raising.

Looking after seedlings

Before nights when frost is forecast, you can lay fleece on top of plant trays on a hot bed to contain more of the warmth, then remove it by day to allow the heap's gentle steam to escape. Otherwise seedlings risk 'damping off' when there is continually moist air trapped by fleece. Likewise, water seedlings in the morning, so that moisture on leaves can evaporate by day, resulting in drier leaves at night, when mildews may otherwise breed.

Eventual emptying

At some point in late autumn or winter, the composted ingredients need emptying out. How to use them then depends on the bedding: when manure contains wood shavings, these decompose slowly in hot beds because there is not a lot of fresh air. In my case they had barely decomposed by December, so I used the contents to mulch some pathways.

Making a hot bed

I made my hot bed with four sheets of plywood, 1.2x1.2m (4x4'). Thin, vertical sides such as this hold in both the contents and some of their heat and, because they are thin, reduce the amount of space needed so can hold more manure, packed tight to their sides and right to the top. I used 1.2cm (½") plywood, with two sheets upright against the greenhouse's brick walls for sides 1 & 2, then hammered a metal stake into soil at the corner opposite, to support sides 3 & 4, with a thin stake in the ground to hold the middle, outer edge of side 3.

I filled the heap from a wheelbarrow through the gap of side 4 by the door, its plywood then put in place after I'd tipped in as much manure as possible. At this point I ran a wire all around, 15cm (6") from the top, starting and finishing at the metal corner post. This holds everything in place, yet makes it quick to assemble and dismantle the bed.

February: filling with fresh horse manure.

Levelling the pallet on top.

Seedlings helped by rising warmth.

March: emptying out after 6 weeks.

Next I jumped up and down on the manure, to firm it as much as possible. Filling was now by fork, up to 1.5m (5') high, before a final dance on top, always pushing manure into the corners to ensure a level surface. A pallet on top makes excellent 'staging' to support plant trays, though sometimes some extra wooden slats are needed, depending on the pallet. Within a day, the heap's temperature was over 40°C (104°F), and first sowings in trays on the pallet germinated well.

February or late winter is a good time for doing this, to get seedlings under way so they can benefit from early spring warmth and lighter days. However, in this particular year, March was continuously freezing, even in the last week, when I was ready to sow warmth-loving seeds such as cucumber, melon and basil. So, 40 days after the first fill, I removed all the hot bed's contents to an outdoor heap and two of us refilled the bed with fresh manure: it took 3 hours, which was a worthwhile investment of time, to keep seeds germinating and frost-tender plants healthy through an unusually cold spring.

Bed refilled with more fresh manure.

Fleece cover on frosty nights.

April: cucumber, melon and courgette.

Late April: strong growth, especially the tomatoes.

Propagation needs of different vegetables

The table opposite gives details of suitable sowing timings and the need for warmth of a range of popular vegetables. These timings are for first and maincrop harvests (see Chapter 10) – you can sow later for later harvests. The estimates for number of weeks to first harvest are for average weather conditions in a zone 9 climate.

The sowing times given are the 'seasonal points' that are good for sowing in temperate climates: if the climate in your area is colder or warmer, you may need to sow earlier or later in the season.

The 'need heat' column gives an indication of the benefit to plant growth and health of giving extra warmth, for germinating and early growth only. A value of 1 means that extra heat is of least benefit, while values from 3 to 5 mean that heat must be given for seeds to germinate evenly at the sowing times given.

The 'weeks on heated bed' time will vary according to how much space you have for all your plants: leaving them on your hot bed or other heated propagating bed for shorter or longer than indicated here is possible, according to ambient temperature. Don't overdo the heat for fast-growing plants such as courgettes, making them ready to plant outside before the weather is warm enough. A value of 1 is for seeds needing just a short burst of warmth to trigger germination; a value of 9 means that both seeds and young plants need constant warmth over a long period.

The 'weeks from sowing to planting' values reflect the likely ambient temperatures when early sowings are made. Any of the vegetables shown here that can also be sown in summer will be ready to plant more quickly, for example lettuce in 3-4 weeks from sowing rather than 5-6.

Sowing and planting direct outside

So many healthy plants can be raised under cover that, once you get the hang of it, outdoor sowing is a less rewarding option. However, some vegetables prefer to be sown direct: the main ones being carrot and parsnip, whose tap roots (the bit we eat, unlike, say, beetroot and swede, whose edible part is a swelling above the tap root) are at risk of forking after being moved. Broad beans also make a long tap root, and they germinate well in cold soil: I find they tend to be healthier when sown direct. Use a dibber to make 5cm (2") holes for their seeds. The same goes for onion sets and garlic cloves. Potatoes too need sowing direct: use a trowel to put seed potatoes 5-10cm (2-4") below surface level, for earthing up later with compost.

Timings and warmth for first vegetables sown under cover

Vegetable*	Sowing time	Need heat	Weeks on heated bed	Weeks from sowing to planting	Time from planting to first harvest
Lettuce for leaves	Late winter	1	2	5-6	4 weeks
Spinach (not beet)	Late winter	1	2	4-5	5-6 weeks
Peas for shoots	Late winter	1	1	3-5	5-6 weeks
Salad (spring) onion	Late winter	1	2	5-6	8 weeks
Onion	Late winter	2	3	5-6	4 months
Parsley / dill / coriander	Late winter	2	3	6-8	5-6 weeks
Early cabbage	Late winter	1	1	5-6	10 weeks
Early calabrese	Late winter	1	1	5-6	12 weeks
Early cauliflower	Late winter	1	1	5-6	12-14 weeks
Beetroot 'Boltardy'	Late winter	2	3	5-6	10-12 weeks
Sweet pepper / chilli pepper	Late winter	5	9	10-13	8-10 weeks
Aubergine	Late winter	5	9	10-13	7-8 weeks
Tomato	Early spring	3	7	8-10	7-8 weeks
Peas for pods	Early spring	1	1	3-4	8-10 weeks
Celery / celeriac	Early spring	2	4	8-9	8-10 weeks
Melon	Early spring	5	6	9-11	9-10 weeks
Cucumber	Mid spring	5	5	5-7	5-6 weeks
Basil	Mid spring	4	6	7-12	6-7 weeks
Sweetcorn	Mid spring	2	2	3-5	15 weeks
Courgette	Mid spring	3	2	4-5	4-5 weeks
Squash	Mid spring	3	2	4-6	4 months
French beans / runner beans	Late spring	3	2	3-4	5-7 weeks

*Vegetables are listed in order of sowing date (i.e. giving a suggested order within the 'seasonal point' of late winter, early spring, etc.), and these timings are to make first plantings ready to go in their final position at a favourable time. For example, I sow tomatoes 4 weeks before cucumbers, because the latter grow faster, then they are ready to plant at the same time.

These carrots were sown into surface compost.

Raising plants outside

A further option is to propagate in the soil outside, with closely sown seeds in drills, for later planting at wider spacings. Here are some good vegetables to try, all in rows (drills) 20cm (8") apart:

- Sow onions for bulbs in early spring (no later), for planting 4-6 weeks later: three seeds per 1cm (8 per 1").
- Sow lettuce from early spring, for planting 4-6 weeks later: two seeds per 1cm (five per 1").
- Sow leeks mid spring, for planting in early summer: two seeds per 1cm (five per 1").
- Sow cabbage, kale, cauliflower and purple sprouting broccoli in spring, according to variety and harvest date: sow seeds 2-3cm (1") apart in the row, and plant out through late spring and early summer.

Sowing into surface compost

When your beds have compost on top, you are sowing (and planting) into this rather than soil. There are some misunderstandings about compost 'burning' seedlings, which is true only for fresh (not composted) manure.

The procedure for sowing into compost is the same as for soil: level with a rake, draw drills, sow seeds, and close the drills. If the compost has just been applied, this still works, as long as it is fine and crumbly. However, if it is recently spread and sticky, you need to wait at least a week before sowing, and until the surface has weathered enough that larger lumps can be broken up with a rake.

The compost you sow into may be lumpier than some soils, but it will still give excellent germination. Consider how readily weed seeds germinate in compost! (See below.) Small lumps of compost are good, because they help to prevent a crust of fine soil forming over germinating seedlings. This is known as 'capping', and can occur when a seedbed is too fine from over-working the soil, preventing any seedlings emerging.

You *can* sow and plant into newly created beds

If you have recently created a bed, for example with compost and well-decomposed manure on top of grass (see Chapter 6), it is possible to sow and plant as soon as weather conditions are right. You don't need to wait for the grass and weeds underneath to die – just make sure that your beds' contents are tamped firm with a spade. It is almost impossible to compact compost, and success is assured when it is firmly held together, rather than too loose and fluffy.

The only time when you need to wait before sowing direct is if the surface compost contains many weed seeds. Either wait until they appear as tiny seedlings, then hoe them off before sowing, or raise your plants under cover, because it is easier to hoe and weed around established plants than close to small seedlings.

Left: Drills drawn in surface compost. Right: After 1 month, carrots and radishes.

CHAPTER TEN

Early sowings and plantings

Waiting for best sowing times; seizing the moment

*"How pleased I am that
I can experience the simple
joy of a person who serves
a cabbage at his table which
he has grown himself."*

Goethe

How early can you start sowing? I think we all have itchy fingers in the late winter and spring, keen to see those first seedlings pop up and say hello to spring. But when I look back on my earlier-than-usual sowings of the past 30 years, very few succeeded. And I lost a lot of seeds. Here are two tips. First, know the best time for first sowings of each vegetable. Second, follow the advice in this chapter on ways to succeed with early sowing.

Some vegetables give their best harvest from a spring sowing, but others do not, and need sowing in summer. In

June: purple sprouting broccoli from a February sowing.

general, the summer solstice marks the boundary between these two groups. This chapter deals with vegetables in the first group, as well as those few that can be sown both in spring and after midsummer. For extra clarity, vegetables covered in this spring-sowings chapter are divided into two types, according to how much they need extra warmth for germination and early growth (see Chapter 9 for more on this).

All the vegetables that are best sown in summer are covered in the next chapter. Their best sowing times are generally after the solstice, to avoid the spring flowering season of these plants. I suggest you buy their seeds in winter or spring to have them ready for summer sowing, helping to keep the ground full all year, giving food most of the time.

Knowing the right time to sow

A good starting point is to keep within the broad time ranges given in the table on page 154. It lists the main vegetables for spring sowing, 2 months earlier indoors than outside, when you have an indoor space for sowing.

In spring, wait to sow; in summer, sow on time

Be wary of advice on seed packets which encourages sowing early, even in milder areas. 'Sow carrots in January and you'll never have to eat

Spinach in May, sown 7 weeks earlier in modules.

carrots', as the saying goes. Some seeds, such as carrot, lettuce and beetroot *can* germinate in cool soil but rarely thrive when attempting to grow in still-cool conditions. Often they are eaten by slugs, buffeted by wind and grow into poor plants.

Throughout spring, the days grow longer and the chance of warmth increases all the time. Using fleece can help early sowings of cool-start vegetables, but not heat-demanding seeds such as French beans, runner beans and sweetcorn: for these, you just need to be patient. If you miss a chance to sow, there will be others.

In summer the opposite is true, because days shorten after the solstice and temperatures drop quickly as summer changes to autumn, so later sowings are at risk of running out of time. Sowing dates in summer are therefore more precise, and by late summer there may be just 1 week of good time to sow certain seeds, after which it is too late. See Chapter 11 for key dates.

Tips for first sowings

Gardening is an exercise in optimism, and to some extent a gamble too, in view of the unknowable weather to come. So – again – don't sow too early in the spring: this way you will reduce potential losses of seeds, plants and time. This advice is hardest to follow in a mild winter and early spring, and occasionally it can be worth sowing earlier than usual, but on the whole, patience pays off.

You just need to ignore those allotment or garden neighbours who brag about having already sown this or that. In spring, later sowings often catch up with early ones, to grow larger and more healthily in the end. See what the neighbours think then!

Spring weather is hugely variable

The effects of weather are often underrated or not explained enough in advice on gardening. For example, in my first year at Homeacres, the cold spring meant waiting a whole month later than usual before sowing outdoors. Sowing dates in spring are a guide only, and if the weather is too cold or wet, you need to wait. In cold weather, raising plants under cover for planting out is more feasible than sowing direct (see below). So:
- Do not sow before the recommended dates.
- If weather is colder than usual, wait until it improves.

Sowings made under cover cope more easily with low temperatures, since they are protected from wind and rain. In early spring they grow slowly but surely, until needing to go out when their roots have filled the modules or pots. Even if the weather is unfavourable, you can plant out and then cover over with fleece.

Using fleece, cloches and minimal hardening off

Fleece covers are easy to use and protect plants from cold wind. The first day of April 2013 in south-west England was a great example of this, with some plants ready to go out but the temperature only just above freezing, at 2°C (36°F), and the wind making it feel even colder.

I brought module trays of lettuce, spinach and onion straight from the unheated greenhouse and we put them into beds without hardening them off. This is possible in spring for four reasons:
- In an unheated structure, nights are cold and plants are used to low temperatures.
- With protection from fleece, plants quickly recover from the brief shock of going into cold soil.
- Fleece creates favourable conditions after planting, in terms of the

Tip: How to use fleece. Laying fleece on plants, rather than supporting it with hoops, keeps any warmth closer to the plants' leaves and roots. It also results in less damage to the fleece, as it is held more securely in place, tight over the bed and firmly on plants' leaves.

temperature of both air and soil, and wind protection, which are significantly more useful than any pre-warming of the soil.

- Rapidly increasing levels of sunshine ensure enough growing time each day for plants to establish well.

I dibbed holes, Steph planted the seedlings, and then we rolled out fleece on top of them, flat over the beds with the cover resting on top of the plants.

The weather continued frosty for another week and with plenty of cold winds all month, but the only damage to these young plants was from leatherjackets eating some roots (see Chapter 3, page 53).

Cool-tolerant vegetables: sowing and planting dates

The sowing, planting and harvest dates for the vegetables described in this section are summarized in the table overleaf, where they are listed in a suggested order of first sowing date. The date ranges given there, and in the table on page 162, are suitable for most of the UK, equivalent in climate to US plant hardiness zones 8-9 – adjust them accordingly if the climate where you live is different. The ranges indicate the earliest possible sowing times, and options to sow later where this is possible.

The 'first harvest' dates in the table give an idea of the likely time for first harvest, based on the dates of first sowing.

See also the table in Chapter 11 (pages 173-4), for second sowings of some vegetables listed here, and of many more vegetables to sow in summer.

Late winter, and holes dibbed for pea plants.

Broad beans

Frost hardy
Spacing: 10x45cm (4x18")
Broad beans are exceptionally hardy as small plants, so seeds can be sown outside in early winter, to grow into seedlings by early spring. Sow from early November, and throughout December in milder areas.

Timing examples for cool-tolerant vegetables				
Vegetable	Sow indoors	Plant out	Sow direct outdoors	First harvest
Broad beans	Dec–Apr	Mar–May	Nov–May	Jun
Lettuce	Feb–Jul	Apr–Aug	Mar–Jul	May
Spinach	Feb–Apr	Mar–May	Mar–Apr	May
Peas for shoots	Feb–Apr	Mar–May	Mar–May	Apr
Onion seeds for salad*	Feb–Aug	Apr–Sep	Mar–Aug	May
Onion, shallot seeds for bulbs	Feb–Mar	Apr	Mar–Apr	Jul
Parsley*	Feb–Jul	Apr–Aug	Mar–Jul	Jun
Coriander*	Feb–Aug	Apr–Sep	Mar–Aug	May
Dill	Feb–Apr	Apr–May	Mar–Apr	May
Early calabrese/cabbage/cauliflower*	Feb–Mar	Apr–May	Mar–Apr	Jun
Beetroot*	Feb–Jun	Apr–Jul	Apr–Jun	Jun
Peas for pods	Mar–May	Apr–Jun	Mar–May	Jun
Potato (first early)			Mar–Apr	Jun
Celery	Mar–May	May–Jul		Jul
Celeriac	Mar	May		Oct
Onion sets, shallot bulbs	Mar	Apr	Apr	Aug
Parsnip			Mar–Jun	Oct
Carrot*			Mar–Jul	Jun
Potato (second early / maincrop)			Apr	Jul / Sep
Leek	late Mar	May–Jun	Apr	Sep
Leaf beet / chard*	Apr–Jul	May–Aug	May–Jul	Jun
Brussels sprouts / autumn cabbage	May	Jun	May	Sep

*Vegetables of two seasons, for sowing early and again in summer (details in Chapter 11).

Even if only half the seeds survive winter, they will tiller (branch) to make more stems and give a worthwhile crop. In milder areas, sow no earlier than the dates given, so that plants are small over winter.

This means early harvests when other vegetables are scarce. Also, it gives you more time to remove the plants after a final pick, then plant another vegetable such as leeks, beetroot, salads or French beans.

Spacings

Many vegetables can be grown equidistantly in blocks, and the spacings given in this and later chapters refer to that method, when I give only one measurement. So 25cm (10") means all plants are that distance from their nearest plants. This is called 'planting on the square'.

Some vegetables grow best in rows: for example climbing beans and peas, which need support; and carrots, which are easiest to sow and grow in lines. I give their spacings as two measurements, hence 10x45cm (4x18") means each plant is the first distance from its nearest neighbour, while the rows are spaced by the second distance.

Both sets of spacings work on beds, but a third possibility is when you grow on flat ground without differentiation into beds. All vegetables are then grown in lines or rows, many of which need space to walk between, which is variable according to how much width you like for access. So in that case you can use my figures as a guide and add some distance according to your preference.

My figures for planting distances are based on long experience and are recommended for giving the most healthy plants and the longest harvest, and for easy access. They are a guide only, and you may wish to vary them.

Lettuce for leaves and hearts

Frost hardy
Spacing: 20-25cm (8-10")
Lettuce can be harvested later for hearts, or earlier for their outer leaves, every week for 3 months until they finally rise to flower. From late winter, sow two seeds per module and thin to the strongest, or in a small tray for pricking seedlings into modules. Plantings at Homeacres on 1 April, from seeds sown indoors in mid February, were covered with fleece for a month, and gave a first harvest on 30 April. The bed was then picked weekly until mid July, by which time most were rising to flower.

Spinach

Frost hardy
Spacing: 15x30cm (6x12") or 25cm (10")
Spinach makes its loveliest, largest, darkest leaves in spring, before flowering at the start of summer, so an early sowing means plants are raring to go as soon as there is a mild spell in spring. Sow two or three seeds per module in late winter to have plants by early spring, plant out and then cover with fleece. You can have an abundance of thick leaves

through late spring, up to a month earlier than from outdoor sowings, until leaves become thinner and paler by mid summer.

Peas

Frost hardy
Spacing for shoots: 25-30cm (10-12")
Spacing for pods: 15x45cm (6x18")
Pea plants are as hardy as broad beans, but more susceptible to bird and slug damage when sown in autumn. They grow most healthily in spring and early summer, from early spring sowings indoors: two or three seeds in pots or modules for about 3 weeks. Outdoor sowing is possible, but mice and birds like pea seeds and shoots. Cover seedlings with fleece or a cloche to keep wind and pigeons off, for 2 or 3 weeks until the plants are growing strongly. For shoots, start picking when plants are 20-30cm (8-12") tall; for peas to eat, support plants with sticks once the fleece or cloche is removed. Leave one or two plants unpicked to dry in situ and give seeds for next year.

Onion and shallot from seed

Frost hardy
Spacing: 30cm (12")
Although onion and shallot seedlings look flimsy and grow slowly at first, they are hardy and turn into sturdy plants by late spring, with fewer

Left: Onion plants in May after fleece is removed. Right: The same plants in July.

problems of disease and bolting than with onions grown from sets. Sow in late winter on a windowsill or under glass, with six onion seeds in every module so that you have clumps of four to six seedlings to plant out in early spring – don't thin them! Covering with fleece for the first month often helps.

Onions swell nicely in each clump, pushing one another apart as they do so. For example, I harvested 4.4kg (9lb 11oz) 'Red Baron' and 4.7kg (10lb 5oz) 'Balaton' yellow onions from just seven modules of each. Shallots grow better in smaller numbers of two or three plants per clump, with each shallot seed making a bulb of two or three segments.

Onions grown from sets.

Onion and shallot from sets/bulbs

Frost hardy
Spacing: 7x30cm (3x12")
Onion sets are baby onions sown the previous summer, and shallot bulbs to plant are one of the several from a previous year's clump. They need less time to mature than onions and shallots from seed: plant shallot bulbs outside in late winter and onion sets in early spring – not before the equinox, or they tend to flower.

Red onions flower more than yellow ones, and at Homeacres I lost a quarter of my Red Baron onions from sets, even though I planted them in April. Shallot bulbs planted in March gave 2kg (4lb 6oz) from a 1.5m (5') row, and I followed them with beetroot.

Parsley, coriander and dill

Frost hardy
Spacing: 20-25cm (8-10")
These are all related umbellifers and, with the exception of curled parsley, flower in summer, so early sowing works well to harvest more leaves before flowering begins. You can sow on a windowsill in mid winter or under cover in late winter, to plant out with a fleece cover for the first

month. For example, my six plants of coriander gave 120g (just over 4oz) weekly throughout late spring.

Early calabrese, cabbage and cauliflower

Frost hardy
Spacing for calabrese / early cabbage: 30-40cm (12-16")
Spacing for cauliflower: 60cm (24")
All these brassicas are hardy and grow well in the cool of early spring: sow from late winter under cover. Grow just a few plants of each, and also sow successively if you want a steady supply, because they tend to come ready at the same time from early summer. Good varieties are an early-hearting cabbage such as 'Greyhound' or 'Derby Day', and an early cauliflower such as 'Snowball', or an F1 hybrid cauliflower such as 'Graffiti' for coloured heads.

Beetroot

Frost hardy
Spacing: 30-40cm (12-16") for clumps
Use 'Boltardy' for early sowings, as other varieties are at risk of flowering when sown before mid spring. Sow four seeds in each module from late winter, for planting in a clump of four seedlings on average, covered with fleece for a month or more. In late spring or early summer, make the first pickings of the largest root in each clump, at whatever size you like to eat them: carefully twist it out and leave the others undisturbed, to continue growing for later harvests.

Potato

Not frost hardy
Spacing: 30-45cm (12-18")
Except for the 'Jersey Royal' (or 'International Kidney'), first earlies are rarely of top flavour, but are good for early-season meals, and avoid potato blight by maturing before it is warm enough for blight spores to multiply. You can pull some surface compost around their new shoots until all risk of frost is passed, or even lay cardboard over them before a frosty night. After June harvests there is time to plant cucumber, leek, kale and cabbage.

Second earlies mature 2 to 4 weeks later, in mid summer. I suggest 'Charlotte' for its high yield of large, waxy tubers, which store well. For floury potatoes, the Sarpo varieties are good. See Chapter 5, pages 79-80, for an example of growing the excellent second early 'Estima'.

Maincrop potatoes continue growing throughout summer and, as long as they escape blight and have enough rain, yields can be high. Try 'King Edward' for top flavour, 'Pink Fir Apple', 'Belle de Fontenay' or 'Anya' for waxy salad tubers, and 'Sarpo Mira' or 'Sarpo Axona' for blight-resistant plants, which will need harvesting by early autumn.

Celery and celeriac

Not frost hardy
Spacing for celery: 30cm (12")
Spacing for celeriac: 40-45cm (15-18")
These tiny seeds want sowing in gentle warmth and with no compost on top of them, as they germinate best in light: cover the tray with glass to keep seeds moist and warm. Then prick seedlings into modules when still small – often you can just see the first true leaves. Plant out after the risk of frost has passed, often 2 months after sowing. Best results come from heavy soils with plenty of organic matter, and some watering in dry weather.

Parsnip

Frost hardy
Spacing: 5x30cm (2x12")
You can sow these at the same time as early carrots, and until late spring. They grow steadily through spring and summer, then become sweeter as the weather cools in autumn. They can be sown into a surface mulch of compost on top of undug soil. Often the roots go deep, making some of them difficult to lever out: use a spade to loosen but not invert the soil.

Carrot

Frost hardy
Spacing: 1x22cm (½x9")
The small seeds and tender seedlings make it wise to wait for milder weather before sowing carrots. If it is mild, this can be in early spring, preferably when the surface has dried a little, because early sowings in wet, cold soil grow more weakly and risk succumbing to slugs. Make the first pullings in early summer, when baby carrots are an exciting new flavour, then you will have larger harvests after the solstice.

Leek

Frost hardy
Spacing: 10x30cm (4x12") for singles, 30cm (12") for clumps
For leeks to harvest in autumn, sow early varieties such as 'Zermatt' and 'Autumn Mammoth'. For leeks to harvest in winter and early spring, grow late varieties such as 'Bandit' and 'Apollo'. Sow in early spring, either three seeds per module or in drills outside (see Chapter 9, page 146). Plant after 1 month for modules or 2 months for plants grown in soil, for harvests over a long period.

Leaf beet and chard

Avoid frost on seedlings
Spacing: 30-37cm (12-15")
Early sowings carry the risk of rising to flower, and best results come from waiting until mid spring for leaf beet and late spring for chard. Sow three seeds per module and either thin to the strongest if you want large leaves, or leave them in clumps of two or three for medium leaves.

Brussels sprouts

Frost hardy
Spacing: 60cm (24")
Brussels' reputation for bitter flavours hides much merit in terms of vitamins, antioxidants and even blood-clotting properties. Sow two seeds per module and thin to the strongest, or prick out seedlings from a tray into modules: sowing in mid spring gives the long season they need. The 60cm spacing looks wide at planting time, and you can plant lettuce in the gaps between, which give company and help the Brussels to grow, as well as providing some extra harvests. F1 Brussels varieties are currently better bred and make tighter buttons, but flavour and harvests are still good if your sprouts 'blow' open, and

Brussels sprout 'Doric' F1 in December.

Cabbage 'Filderkraut' in October.

'flower sprouts' (a cross between Brussels and kale) are another option, with pretty rosettes of pink-red leaves.

Autumn cabbage

Frost hardy
Spacing: 45-50cm (18-20")
Sow and plant these at the same time as your Brussels, but a difference is that you must keep caterpillars off with mesh or 5mm (⅛") black netting. Outer leaves are often nibbled by slugs and insects, but hearts kept insect-free under fine netting or mesh make a great autumn harvest and can be stored through winter, kept cool and frost-free, ideally at 2-5°C (36-41°F). There is a huge choice of pointed or round varieties, which mostly need at least 4 months to make a firm heart: check the details on the seed packet.

Warmth-demanding vegetables: sowing and planting dates

The plants in this group are all killed by frost, and their seeds need high temperatures to germinate – up to 30°C (86°F). Then the seedlings like steady warmth of 15-25°C (59-77°F), so seeds are best sown later rather than sooner in the season, in order that the growing plants can be accommodated in suitable conditions. For example, it is easy to germinate tomatoes on a windowsill in winter, but you then need an ever-larger space

Timing examples for warmth-demanding vegetables				
Vegetable	Sow indoors	Plant out	Sow direct outdoors	First harvest
Pepper / chilli pepper / aubergine	Feb–Mar	Jun		Aug
Tomato	Mar–Apr	Jun		Aug
Melon	Mar to early Apr	Jun		Aug
Cucumber	Mar–May	Jun	Jun	Jul
Sweetcorn	Apr–May	May-Jun	May	Sep
Courgette	Apr–May	May-Jun	May	Jun
Squash (summer)	Apr	May-Jun	May	Jul
Squash (winter) / pumpkin	Apr	May-Jun	May	Sep
Summer beans	May–Jun	Jun-Jul	Late May to Jun	Jul

in which to keep the fast-growing plants, which can't go outside until late spring. Greenhouses and polytunnels are good for early sowing as long as you have a heat source to protect plants in frosty weather.

Sowing, planting and harvest dates for these vegetables are summarized in the table above; the crops listed in suggested order of first sowing date.

While some of those in this group (courgette, squash, sweetcorn and beans) are generally planted outdoors in temperate climates, others can be grown under cover for their whole season, and some (melon, sweet and chilli peppers, aubergine) need this protection for successful ripening – in the UK at least. See Chapter 13 for more about growing under cover and about many of the vegetables listed here.

Pepper, chilli pepper and aubergine

Spacing: 45-50cm (18-20")
These are similar to tomatoes (see below) but are slower-growing: sow 2-4 weeks earlier, and extra heat is needed, especially for good germination and early growth. It is worth buying young plug plants if you want only a small number, then pot on until they're ready for planting.

Tomato

Spacing: 45-50cm (18-20")
Sow in early spring for tomatoes to grow under cover, and a month later for tomatoes to grow outdoors. You can germinate seeds in a small seed

tray and allow the seedlings to grow for a fortnight or more, until you see the first true leaf, then use a pencil to lift the roots out and plant them deeply into small pots of compost. Bury the stem up to the lowest green leaf, as when pricking out any vegetable seedlings, to make sturdier plants.

I sow my tomatoes in trays above a hot bed in the green-house (see Chapter 9, page 141), where they grow slowly but surely through cool spring weather. There is enough warmth from the decompos-ing manure to keep night frost away, although I cover plants

The outdoor tomato 'Gardener's Delight' in September.

with fleece if it is forecast to be below -4°C (25°F) outside.

Then, in a greenhouse or polytunnel, you can plant just before or as soon as the last frost date has passed. Wait until early summer for outdoor plantings; for example, I set three 'Sungold' tomatoes in bags of soil and compost in June, against a south-facing wall, and they cropped steadily through summer (see Chapter 5, page 82).

Melon and cucumber

Spacing: 60cm (24")
These also need steady warmth, and do best when you can keep them growing steadily all the time, so there is no need to sow any earlier than the spring equinox. I sow a week after the equinox, for indoor cucumber and melon, and up to a month after that for outdoor cucumbers.

Sweetcorn

Spacing: 30cm (12")
Sweetcorn is easy to grow and can reward you with superb flavours. Do not be tempted to sow before mid spring indoors – plants set out by early summer have enough time to grow well. Expensive hybrid seed is worth every penny, especially of supersweet varieties, for the extra sweetness it

Courgettes in their own new bed.

has compared with open-pollinated varieties. Also, the corn stays sweeter for longer after picking.

Courgette, squash and pumpkin

Spacing: 60cm (24")

These have large seeds and grow rapidly, so there's no need to sow before mid spring under cover, and 2 to 3 weeks later outdoors, depending on when your last frost generally occurs. The last frost here is around mid May, so I sow under cover 3-4 weeks before that; then, after planting, I sometimes cover them with fleece for 3 weeks if there are cold winds.

For winter squash, an excellent variety is the attractive dark orange 'Uchiki Kuri' or 'Red Kuri', which has many useful attributes:

- Plants grow an average four fruit per plant, of about 1kg (2lb 3oz) each.
- Fruits usually ripen by early autumn, and store well, often until March.
- They have a flavour as sweet and a texture as dense as other good varieties, such as 'Buttercup', 'Crown Prince' and 'Sweet Dumpling'.

Most butternut winter squash need a warmer climate than that of the UK, and in cool summers they fail to thrive, then run out of time to ripen.

Pumpkins need extra space to ramble, making large fruits that are less sweet and store less well than winter squash.

Summer squash include crooknecks, pattypans and courgettes. Harvest regularly, and mature fruits will store for 1-3 months.

Borlotti and runner beans in September.

Climbing summer beans and dwarf French beans

Spacing for climbing beans: 30x60cm (12"x24")
Spacing for dwarf French beans: 40cm (16")

These beans are easily checked by cool weather, so avoid sowing too early. Sow under cover in mid spring and outdoors in early summer.

For green beans, you can make two sowings of dwarf French varieties such as 'Castandel': one seed in each module. The first sowing is made in late spring, for planting early summer and cropping for 6-8 weeks. Then a second sowing, around the solstice, will crop in late summer, by which time the first sowing will be giving sporadic harvests.

Alternatively, you can have French beans all summer from just one sowing of the climbing French bean 'Cobra'.

A third option is to grow borlotti and runner beans, leaving them unpicked until autumn, when the pods are drying to yellow or brown and are full of beans. After picking and podding, spread the beans on trays in a warm place to finish drying indoors, then keep in jars until needed. This gives a store of nutritious winter food and they are delicious too: 'Czar' runner beans, for example, are like butter beans, only creamier and full of flavour. Furthermore, you automatically have seed for the following spring and I find that germination is close to 100 per cent.

CHAPTER ELEVEN

Successional sowings and plantings

Timing is key for continuing abundance as the season wanes

"There comes a time when autumn asks,'What have you been doing all summer?'"

Anon.

Sowing in summer expands your growing space by keeping it full, and the new vegetables help to keep soil clean of weeds. Perhaps the only downside is the challenge of fitting in a summer holiday: if you are away while seeds need sowing, sow as soon as possible on returning, or you could ask a gardening neighbour to make some sowings for you. This chapter follows on from Chapter 10, with growing advice and best timings to make the most of what your garden has to offer.

Advantages of summer sowings

There are three, interlinked benefits of summer sowings: fewer weeds, vegetables to harvest through autumn and beyond, and a more rewarding scene in the garden as the season wanes.

When vegetable roots are growing in the soil, and their leaves are using the light which would otherwise fall on it, there are fewer opportunities for weeds to grow. You still need to weed, but it's quicker. Do continue looking for and removing any weeds, among the leaves of summer and autumn vegetables, to be sure that none sets seed, as this also reduces the need for weeding in future.

Summer sowings give so many extra harvests. Up to half of what you pick in autumn can be from plants sown in summer, and many wonderful flavours come from summer sowings, such as those of sugarloaf chicory, bulb fennel and chervil. There are also some vegetables to sow in autumn, for harvests in the spring hungry gap.

As well as being more productive and weed suppressing, keeping the

October: these are July sowings of spinach (left) and chervil (right).

ground full creates a feast for the eye, with beautiful vegetables to admire. Gardeners who come on courses at Homeacres in autumn are amazed at the abundance of continuing growth, and love seeing the promise of harvests to come.

A busy halfway point

Summer is a time of maximum activity, for both plants and gardeners: a chance to harvest, clear and re-stock with more seeds and plants, to make the most of soil that is buzzing with life, all its nutrients available. There is still plenty of light, and a reservoir of soil warmth that lasts into autumn.

After any final harvests in early summer, remove plants straight away and sow on the same day, or set out plants that have been growing elsewhere, to make the most of summer's growth potential. When you have raised plants ready to pop in after clearing, instead of sowing direct, you are extending the growing season by the amount of time they have already spent growing in modules or a seedbed.

Tips for second croppings

Compared with spring, the rhythm of summer is faster, time is precious, and you must seize every possible opportunity to keep up to date. A no-dig approach helps enormously, because there is no requirement to work the ground.

The garden is still full in November.

No soil preparation

You can leave the soil alone between clearing and planting, except for a little treading or raking to firm lumps that may have arisen when pulling out a first vegetable. The compost spread in winter provides enough soil vitality and slow-release nutrients for second crops to prosper. This makes second sowings and plantings quick and simple, when time is precious.

An exception to this is if you have spread little or no compost in winter or spring, in which case a light covering of 1-2cm (½-1") can be spread in summer before new plantings.

Two moves

1. Quick clear. At the earliest opportunity, clear all remains of vegetables after a last harvest, and any weeds, so you have clear soil. For example, pull out spinach when plants start to flower; pull or cut the stems of broad beans and peas as you take the last few pods; twist out lettuce stumps straight after their final harvest. In dry weather, walk on cleared soil to smooth it over and break up any lumps, or if it's wet, use a rake to level the top 3cm (1").
2. Quick plant. Be ready with seeds for plants to go in the same day after clearing. Unlike in spring, punctuality is of the essence in summer sowing, because light is decreasing and temperatures are going to drop. Each day in July is worth roughly 2 days in August, 4 in September, 8 in October and half the month of November!

Crop rotation

Different plants – all brassicas.

It is widely recommended that the position of vegetables in a plot is rotated over time, in order to minimize build-ups of pests and disease and to vary the nutrient demands on the soil. The governing principle of crop rotation is plant family relationships (see table opposite): the aim being to grow plants of a different family from the previous crop in a given area. Advice on rotation normally talks in years, and assumes one planting per year, so if you are gardening with successive croppings in the same year, this means looking at rotation differently.

Summer sowings shorten plant rotation periods if the second vegetable is of a different family from the first, for example leeks after potatoes or kale after garlic. You are then doing 2 'years' of rotation in 1 year. Supposing that in the following year you grew lettuce followed by French beans, you would then have condensed 4 'years' of rotation into just 2 years.

Alternatively, you could grow a second vegetable of the same family, to complete one whole year of, say, brassicas. For example, kale after early cabbage and French beans after broad beans.

In short, the practice of rotation is just one part of maintaining healthy soil and growing vibrant plants. If I were short of space, I would not forego a second planting because it did not fit a rotation plan.

Plant families	
Family	Vegetables and common herbs
Alliums (Alliaceae)	Chives, garlic, leek, onion, salad onion, shallot
Asparagaceae	Asparagus
Beets (Chenopodiaceae)	Beetroot, chard, leaf beet, orach, spinach
Brassicas (Brassicaceae)	Broccoli, Brussels sprouts, cabbage, cauliflower, kohl rabi, land cress, oriental leaves, radish, rocket, swede, turnip
Cucurbits (Cucurbitaceae)	Courgette, cucumber, melon, squash
Grasses (Poaceae)	Sweetcorn (also bamboo, cereals)
Legumes (Fabaceae)	Broad beans, French beans, runner beans, peas
Lettuces / daisies (Asteraceae)	Artichoke (globe and Jerusalem), chicory, endive, lettuce
Mints (Lamiaceae)	Basil, Chinese artichoke, marjoram, mint, rosemary, sage, thyme
Oxalis (Oxalidaceae)	Oca, sorrel (also dock/rumex)
Polygonaceae	Rhubarb
Solanums (Solanaceae)	Aubergine, chilli pepper, pepper, potato, tomato
Umbellifers (Umbelliferae)	Carrot, celery, celeriac, chervil, coriander, dill, fennel, parsley, parsnip
Valerianaceae	Corn salad (lamb's lettuce)

Intersowing and interplanting

This is a bonus option – a fun way of speeding things up and increasing harvests. It matches the slowly increasing growth of seedlings with the declining needs of maturing plants. After a careful harvest of the latter, with minimal soil disturbance, you are rewarded with rapid growth of the second sowing or planting. Here are a few examples.

- An early summer sowing of beetroot in modules, four plants in each, can be planted between maturing shallots, onion sets or garlic in late June. The alliums come out soon after, you may need to water the beetroot if it is dry, and at Homeacres I harvested some medium-sized beetroot on 30 July, only 3 weeks after harvesting shallots.
- You can also sow beetroot and carrots direct in early summer, between rows of maturing garlic.
- Kale and purple sprouting broccoli grow well from interplanting, when sown in early summer and planted 4 weeks later between early salads, chard, garlic, shallots and lettuce. I planted kale between garlic in early July and it established while the garlic matured, then grew strongly from August until spring. Leeks planted between lettuce in late May grew large by the end of summer.

- Lamb's lettuce is ideal for intersowing, because it germinates and grows so slowly. Sow in late summer between young plants of Florence fennel or regularly picked lettuce, to mature through late autumn and winter, after careful clearance of the first vegetables.
- You can make late summer sowings and plantings of land cress, chervil, coriander and wild rocket just as for lamb's lettuce.

Broccoli planted between chard: May (top) and July (bottom).

Sowing and planting dates

The table below gives suitable date ranges for summer sowings of vegetables. Vegetables are listed in suggested order of first sowing date. As with the other date-specific information in this book, these timings are for the climate at Homeacres, so you may need to adjust them for where you live (see page 153). More details for each vegetable follow: the spacings given are mostly equidistant for planting in beds, with some double figures for sowing direct in rows (see box in Chapter 10, page 155.)

Timings for summer- and autumn-sown vegetables

Vegetable	Sow in modules/trays	Plant out	Sow direct outdoors?*	Harvest
Kale	May–Jun	Late Jun to Jul	May–Jun	Sep–May
Swede	Late May to early Jun	Late Jun	Late May to early Jun, best under cover	Oct–Apr
Purple sprouting broccoli	May–Jul	Jun–Aug	No	Feb–May
Calabrese	Jun	Jul	No	Oct–Nov
Cabbage, not spring	Jun	Jul	No	Oct–Apr
Cauliflower	Jun	Jul	No	Mar–May
French beans	Jun	Early Jul	Jun	Aug–Oct
Beetroot	Jun to early Jul	Jul	Jun	Sep–Dec
Carrot	Jun to early Jul	No	Jun	Sep–Nov
Lettuce	Early Jun to mid Jul	Late Jun to early Aug	Early Jun to mid Jul	Jul–Nov leaves; Aug–Oct hearts
Florence fennel	Jun–Jul	Jul–Aug	Jun to early Jul	Sep–Oct
Endive & chicory for leaves	Mid Jun to Aug	Aug–Sep	Mid Jun to Aug	Sep–Apr
Chicory, hearting	Jul 1-20	Aug	No	Oct–Nov
Endive, hearting	Jul to early Aug	Aug	No	Sep–Nov
Parsley	Jul	Aug–Sep	Jul	Sep–May
Chard	Jul	Aug	Jul	Sep–Nov
Wild rocket	Jul	Aug	Jul	Sep–Jun

*Where 'no', this is because too much space is needed for germinating seeds and seedlings at wide spacings, often at a time when a preceding vegetable is still growing.

(Table cont'd overleaf)

Timings for summer- and autumn-sown vegetables

Vegetable	Sow in modules/trays	Plant out	Sow direct outdoors?*	Harvest
Coriander / chervil	Jul to early Aug	Aug	Jul	Sep–Apr
Land cress	Jul to early Aug	Aug	Jul to early Aug	Oct–May
Spinach	Jul–Aug	Aug to early Sep	Jul–Aug	Sep–May
Chinese cabbage	Late Jul	Aug	No	Oct–Nov
Oriental leaves	Aug	Aug–Sep	Aug	Sep–Apr
Salad rocket	Aug	Aug–Sep	Aug	Sep–Apr
Winter purslane	Aug	Aug–Sep	Aug	Oct–Apr
Spring cabbage	Late Aug	Sep	No	Apr–Jun
Onion seeds	Late Aug	Sep	Late Aug	Mar–Jul
Lamb's lettuce	Late Aug to early Sep	Sep	Late Aug to early Sep	Nov–Apr
Onion sets	Oct	Oct–Nov	Oct, best sown direct	Jun–Jul
Garlic	Oct–Dec	Nov–Mar	Oct–Dec, best sown direct	Jun–Jul

*Where 'no', this is because too much space is needed for germinating seeds and seedlings at wide spacings, often at a time when a preceding vegetable is still growing.

Kale

Spacing: 45cm (18")
'Redbor' F1 is pretty and gives high yields, while 'Cavolo Nero' has more tender, dark green leaves of fine flavour but lower yield. 'Hungry Gap' is excellent for continuing to grow through spring with tender new leaves. Kale is tough and tolerates much pest damage in summer, then grows healthy new leaves from autumn when summer pests are hibernating.

Swede

Spacing: 37cm (15")
Sow two seeds per module in late spring, thin to the strongest seedling after 10 days and plant after spinach, for example, when plants are 4 weeks old. As they grow, pull off any yellowing leaves, which otherwise accumulate slugs underneath. Swede makes large plants in damp, heavy soil with plenty of organic matter, giving dense and extremely frost-hardy roots: a great food for winter.

June plantings of swede and kale.

Purple sprouting broccoli for spring cropping

Spacing: 60cm (24")

Make sure your seed packet says it is for spring harvest, because there are now varieties of purple sprouting that crop a few months after sowing. For varieties to crop in or after late winter, you can sow in mid spring and have huge plants by autumn, or sow in early summer to plant after many spring harvests; for example, I planted on 14 July, straight after harvesting second early potatoes. There are varieties such as 'Late Purple Sprouting', for picking through the hungry gap in spring, and F1 hybrids such as 'Mendocino', which can be sown in mid summer for late plantings.

Calabrese

Spacing: 45cm (18")

Sow in early summer for heads in autumn, but calabrese needs good protection from butterflies, as caterpillars love the heads in autumn. Slugs may also become involved in damp autumn weather.

Cabbage

Spacing: 45cm (18")

From early summer sowings, you can have cabbage hearts any time from mid autumn to spring, depending on variety and weather. I grew 'Christmas

A July planting of dwarf French beans (in middle).

Drumhead' after early potatoes, and despite the name there were decent hearts by October, which then started to split and needed eating. For winter hearts you can sow savoy cabbages, which firm up more slowly and are the most frost-hardy type.

Cauliflower

Spacing: 45-60cm (18-24")
An early summer sowing, to plant after spring vegetables, makes large plants by autumn, which stand through winter and make curds in spring. Be sure to grow a variety that is bred for this, such as 'Aalsmeer', which tolerates frost and then develops its curd in milder weather.

French beans

Spacing: 40cm (16")
Early summer sowings in modules give plants ready to go out in just 2 weeks, and you can sow dwarf beans at the summer solstice. In a mild autumn French beans crop for a long time.

Beetroot

Spacing: 30cm (12")
Beetroot grows fast and is extremely useful as a second crop (see page 172). When moisture and organic matter are in good supply, large roots are not woody: we made salad for 20 people from a single root. The small roots of mid-summer sowings have healthy young leaves, good for eating in salads.

Carrot

Spacing: 3x30cm (1x12")
Early summer is best for sowing winter carrots, such as 'Berlicum' and 'Autumn King'. You can also sow the faster-maturing 'Early Nantes' in mid summer for eating through autumn, covered with mesh to keep out carrot root fly.

Lettuce

Spacing: 20-25cm (8-10")
Sow and grow as for spring sowings (see Chapter 10, page 155), except that you may notice more pests and disease, such as root aphids and mildew, because lettuce is less 'in season' by late summer and autumn, when it is normally flowering. Hence my advice is to grow relatively less lettuce at this time, and sow more endive, chicory, rocket, land cress and oriental leaves.

Florence (bulb) fennel

Spacing: 30cm (12")
Because Florence fennel flowers in late spring, it is best sown at or after summer solstice. My main sowing was on 20 July, planted 4 weeks later after clearing spring lettuce, and there were lovely bulbs for harvesting throughout October. Then in late summer I sowed lamb's lettuce between the six rows of fennel plants (see photo on page 181) and enjoyed many cuts of these leaves from late autumn and through winter.

Endive and chicory leaves

Spacing: 10x30cm (4x12") or 20cm (8")
Picked regularly of their outer leaves, as for lettuce, endive and chicory can be productive over a long period. The scarole endive 'Elysee' sown in early summer can be picked for up to 3 months. Other good varieties are 'Bubikopf' for broad leaves, 'Fine Maraichere' and 'Frenzy' for finer, frisée leaves.

Chicory hearts

Spacing: 35cm (14")
These grow best from sowing in the month after solstice, for hearting in autumn, with a final harvest before any frosts below about -3°C (27°F).

Sown in July, these chicory hearts are good by November.

Sow in seed trays and prick small seedlings into modules, or sow two seeds per module and thin to the strongest. Plant out after harvests of onions, calabrese and second early potatoes, for hearts over several weeks in autumn. Franchi Seeds offers good varieties, and I recommend 'Palla Rossa' for earlier harvests and 'Marzatica' for long-keeping, red hearts. Sugarloaf chicories grow large, with some firm-hearted plants and some quite open; the latter are fine to leave out in hard frost. Alternatively, the flowering puntarelle chicories have broccoli-like buds, harvested before frost in autumn, from sowing in early-to-mid summer.

Endive hearts

Spacing: 30cm (12")
Endive grows fast and its hearts do not stand for long before rotting, so be ready to harvest once they look full and are self-blanching in the middle: cut all leaves, but above the smallest heart, for good regrowth. Sow 'Bubikopf' and 'Fine Maraichere' soon after the solstice and they will be ready by early autumn, with a second cut in late autumn. Or pick outer leaves as for lettuce (see 'Endive and chicory leaves', page 177).

Parsley

Spacing: 20-25cm (8-10")
Summer sowings give stronger plants than spring sowings, for picking through the winter months. Parsley is slow to germinate, even in summer, so keep the seed tray moist and be patient. Prick seedlings into modules

and plant out at the end of summer to have leaves through the autumn, with plants sometimes surviving winter too, especially if cloched.

Chard

Spacing: 37cm (15")
Spring sowings of chard often flower by early summer, especially in the case of ruby chard, so early summer is a great time to sow, with up to four seeds per module. Thin seedlings to one plant per module, for large leaves, or three plants per module for smaller leaves for salad. Growth is rapid from summer plantings, and cropping is over a long period, even until spring if the winter is not severe. Chard can be planted even in late summer and looks picturesque in the autumn garden.

Wild rocket

Spacing: 22cm (9")
You can sow direct in mid summer, even intersow between onions as they finish growing, with only a few plants needed for lots of leaves. Module sowing works well: drop a small pinch of the tiny seeds in modules and thin to two or three seedlings in each, for planting in late summer and a first pick in early autumn. Cut leaves horizontally across the top, or snip around the edges, or pick a few leaves through autumn, then roots go dormant in winter before springing back with new growth.

Coriander and chervil

Spacing: 20-25cm (8-10")
Sow direct, or in modules to transplant. If you have tried sowing chervil only in the spring, you will be amazed how easily it grows from sowing in summer, with plentiful leaves through autumn and also in early spring, if it survives winter. Coriander flowers less from summer than spring sowing, and withstands freezing, but does not like cold winds or incessant rain.

Land cress

Spacing: 5x30cm (2x12")
For a brassica, the seeds are small, and seedlings are as slow to develop as wild rocket, so midsummer sowings give plants of a good size by early autumn. Leaves taste peppery; you need only a few plants and have the option to pick larger leaves, or cut across the top. Land cress grows in cold weather and survives winter in the open, with a net to keep pigeons off.

Spinach

Spacing: 15x30cm (6x12") or 25cm (10")
The leaves of summer-sown spinach, growing in damp autumnal conditions, often have slug holes, but the plants are hardy and survive much frost. 'Medania' is a good variety to sow in modules, with two seeds thinned to one plant, for harvests through autumn and often again in spring.

Chinese cabbage

Spacing: 37cm (15")
This is a fast-growing oriental leaf but needs special care. Sow in mid summer only (late July in the UK), and you must cover plants with fleece or mesh to keep insects out, because they *all* love Chinese cabbage! I planted in August, between and at the same time as purple sprouting broccoli, all under mesh. From eleven plants I harvested seven hearts in November, following slug damage to the other four.

Oriental leaves

Spacing: 15-30cm (6x12") or 22cm (9")
These are easy, fast plants to grow, with so many colours, shapes and flavours. When sown in late summer their leaves are healthier than from spring sowings and crop for longer, throughout autumn at least. Sowing in late summer is possible in milder areas, either direct or in module trays for planting out within 3 weeks. In mild autumns they give harvests of excellent quality and quantity. Try 'Red Frills' mustard for its deep colour, abundance of growth and mild but peppery flavour. Mustards and leaf radish are easier to grow than pak choi, which tends to attract slugs.

Salad rocket

Spacing: 15-30cm (6x12") or 22cm (9")
Sow and space as for oriental leaves, to harvest healthy leaves all through autumn, with plants often surviving until spring, especially when sown near the end of summer.

Winter purslane

Spacing: 10x30cm (4x12") or 20cm (8")
The slow growth of spindly seedlings and soft, fleshy leaves belie the plants' hardiness, but they are difficult to grow for quality leaves without

some holes, brown patches and flowering stems. I find that growing under a cloche is good, placed over plants in late autumn. Harvest by cutting larger leaves around the perimeter, handling plants gently because their rooting is so shallow and easily disturbed.

Spring cabbage

Spacing: 30cm (12")
Plant out in early autumn, so they have time to establish before winter. They are most likely to survive cold weather as small plants, which then heart in spring. You need to mesh or net against pigeons and remove slug-infested, lower leaves in March.

Onion from seed

Spacing: 10x30cm (4x12") for bulbs or 20cm (8") for salad onions
The last week of summer is sowing time, for both bulb and spring onion to overwinter: check the seed packet says this is possible for the variety, such as 'Senshyu Yellow' (bulb) and 'White Lisbon' for salads. The latter can be spaced more closely, as they are pulled in the spring before bulbing. I sow in modules, six seeds for bulb and up to ten for salad onion, for planting in late September.

Lamb's lettuce

Spacing: 5x30cm (2x12") or 12cm (5")
You can sow in modules, two seeds thinned to one plant, or sow direct, as described on page 172 and for Florence fennel (page 177). Often it is dry at the right time of year for sowing direct, so after drawing a drill, water into it carefully (to moisten the drill only), then after sowing, pull dry soil on top, to help conserve moisture around the germinating seeds. Harvests of mild-tasting heads of lamb's lettuce throughout winter are small but welcome.

September: lamb's lettuce seedlings emerging between fennel.

Summer caterpillars

In a hot summer there is significant caterpillar damage to leaves of all brassicas – namely the first six plants on pages 174-6, plus oriental leaves, salad and wild rocket and land cress. For plants such as purple sprouting broccoli and kale, whose harvests are later, this is not a problem as long as the plants survive, which they mostly do. But for decent harvests in autumn of brassica salad leaves and cabbage hearts, you need to cover with either fleece, black netting of 5-7mm (¼-⅜") gauge or preferably white mesh, because this also excludes other possible pests such as midges and weevils.

Onion from sets

Spacing: 10x30cm (4x12")
These are quicker to plant, and are planted later, than bulb onions from seed; for example, you can pop them in after runner beans or courgettes, then cover with 3cm (1") of compost.

Garlic

Spacing: 10x45cm (4x18") or 15cm (6")
Mid autumn onwards is good for sowing: choose larger cloves and then cover with 3cm (1") compost. I have kept my own seed for 15 years, of unknown name, and it is as healthy as ever, bulbs growing large when the weather is fair in early summer. For top flavour, 'Solent Wight' gives smaller bulbs which are tasty in salads; they mature a fortnight later in midsummer.

Sowing green manure in early autumn

A green manure is any plant that is sown and grown when soil would otherwise be bare, usually in autumn after clearing a crop. The idea is to add organic matter in a cheap and simple way, and to give soil cover, although this can also lead to some weeds seeding and slugs increasing.

Sometimes in a situation where you have bare soil, you can plant more vegetables, or you could scatter seed of fast-growing ones such as salad rocket, mizuna and edible mustards. When soil is fertile, it is more worth-while to sow and plant vegetables than to sow green manure in late

Mid October. This mustard was sown 40 days earlier.

summer, but if you have any spare areas in early autumn, white mustard (*Sinapis alba*) is a useful choice for green manure. It grows fast, increases organic matter in the soil, and does not need digging in, because it will be killed by winter frosts.

For example, in the experiment described in Chapter 8, where I used no compost, some of the soil was going to be bare for many months. So after the harvest of winter squash, and pulling the few small weeds, I scattered seed of white mustard in early September and lightly raked it in. This mustard grows up to 90cm (36") tall by winter, when it is killed by frosts below about -5°C (23°F), solving any problem of how to remove it before spring plantings, although you may need to pull out a few survivors. Mostly it leaves a debris of dry stems on the surface, and you can either rake them off or plant through them.

I sowed mustard on my new asparagus bed too, which had some large gaps from poor establishment. The mustard's fast-growing roots until the arrival of frosts kept soil alive, and the plants had decayed to straw-like stems by the time I filled gaps with new asparagus plants in early spring.

CHAPTER TWELVE

One bed, one year

An example of sowing, re-sowing and yields from a single bed

"No occupation is so delightful to me as the culture of the earth, and no culture comparable to that of the garden."

Thomas Jefferson

This chapter pulls together many things – sowing, propagating, growing, weeding and harvesting – demonstrated in a single bed over the course of 1 year, to give ideas for managing a growing space throughout a season. It conveys a sense of which vegetables you can plant early, which ones grow well together, how far apart they need to be, and what plantings are possible after which harvests.

The bed

The bed in question is the undug bed of my dig/no-dig experiment, featured in Chapter 7. It measures 1.5x5m (5x16') and has oak sides. It was quick to create: the sides and ends are simply sitting on level ground, pasture at the time, screwed together with corner braces but not fixed to the soil. I filled it in December with 1¼ tons of 18-month-old composted cow manure – to a depth of 20cm (8").

This gave a slightly lumpy surface for sowing and planting into, as I did not have enough fine compost to create a smooth layer on top. However, broad beans, carrots and parsnips germinated well from direct sowing, while everything else was sown into modules and then set out as plants.

Weeds

There were some energetic perennial weeds below the compost; part of the matted root pattern of old pasture. New leaves of these perennial weeds popped up through spring and early summer, and were regularly removed with a trowel. Also, a small flush of seedling weeds appeared in April, mostly grass and clover, which I either pulled out individually or dispersed en masse when tiny, with the blade of a trowel, taking care to avoid disturbing young vegetable seedlings.

Tip: Stay on top of the weeds. As noted in earlier chapters, it is important to keep looking for new weed growth and deal with it as soon as seen, simply because small weeds are quicker and easier to remove than large ones. Also, this gives less time for new leaves of perennial weeds, such as couch grass, to feed energy back to their roots, so that they die more quickly – by the end of summer in this case.

Plantings on the first day of April were then covered with fleece.

First crops

I sowed broad beans on a mild Christmas Day. The first leaves appeared a month later, and plants stayed as seedlings through the coldest March ever. If their stems had been taller they would have suffered frost damage.

Next in were shallots and 'Swift' first early potatoes, early in March, while most of the action was in the greenhouse, with young plants growing in modules from February sowings. They went into dibbed holes through April, together with direct sowings of carrots and parsnips. From 1 April to 16 May, the bed was covered with fleece to protect plants from strong and cold winds, except for the broad beans, which are so hardy. The table below lists the crops in order of their arrival in the bed, as seeds or plants.

First crops							
Vegetable	Sown	Planted	Number of plants	Harvest	Yield		Followed with*
					kg	lb/oz	
Broad bean 'Aquadulce'	Dec		26	Early Jul	5.01	11lb 1oz	French bean
Shallot 'Red Sun'	Mar		10	Early Jul	2.55	5lb 10oz	Beetroot
Coriander / dill	Feb	Apr	8	May–Jun	0.47	1lb	Celery
Spinach 'Toscane'	Feb	Apr	8	May–Jun	2.41	5lb 5oz	Swede

*See table on page 191. (Table cont'd overleaf)

First crops							
Vegetable	Sown	Planted	Number of plants	Harvest	Yield		Followed with*
					kg	lb/oz	
Lettuce leaves, mixed	Feb	Apr	24	May–Aug	9.87	21lb 12oz	Leek
Onion 'Balaton'	Feb	Apr	36	Aug	5.55	12lb 4oz	Endive
Onion 'Red Baron'	Feb	Apr	36	Aug	4.69	10lb 6oz	Endive
Carrot 'Nantes'	Apr		50	Jun–Jul	3.26	7lb 3oz	Celery
Beetroot 'Boltardy'	Feb	Apr	32	Jun–Jul	3.57	7lb 14oz	Fennel
Cabbage 'Greyhound'	Feb	Apr	5	Jun	3.70	8lb 3oz	Kale
Potato 'Swift' (first early)	Mar		5	Jun	2.36	5lb 3oz	Cucumber / leek
Parsnip 'Tender and True'	Apr		22	Nov	7.15	15lb 12oz	None

*See table on page 191.

A lull

With everything sown and planted by mid April, the only input needed in the next month was weekly weeding with a trowel, which took about half an hour – more than normal because of the perennial weeds trying to re-grow. Once you have soil clean of perennial weeds, there is so little time needed for weeding – though always little and often, and this regular attention is also a chance to keep an eye on the progress of the vegetables, and notice things such as when beans need support from the wind.

The two main jobs through the rest of the early part of the year are picking every few days, and clearing of crop residues such as bean stems and cabbage stalks, before replanting in summer.

Early harvests

The first harvests were spinach and some outer leaves of the lettuce, in early May. I pick weekly because of how I market the produce, but you could pick these leaves more frequently, especially in warm weather when they grow faster. The important thing is to pick regularly, which results in a steady flow of food, through late spring and early summer in this case.

May is a lean month for harvests and is the main 'hungry gap' period. June turns into a joyful time of new harvests and exciting flavours, with

Tip: Happy harvesting habits. Have two containers when harvesting, one for the produce and one for everything else – reject vegetables, weeds and slugs. The welcome result is that after every harvest, soil and plants are clean, with less habitat for pests. My trusty 'compost bucket' is a constant garden companion for almost everything I do, and all its contents go on the compost heap, including slugs: I have not noticed them slither out, or any extra damage near the heaps. Harvest leaf and fruiting vegetables even when you don't need them. Friends love such a gift. Whereas if left unpicked, leafy plants in particular go from high-quality to sub-standard leaves within a few days, while beans go tough and seedy.

first harvests of vegetables such as beetroot, carrots, peas, calabrese, and the first courgettes and broad beans.

Yields from first sowings

The record of harvests reflects the hungry gap in May, when there were only leaves to eat, with just 4kg (nearly 9lb) of harvests. June was more abundant, especially when the root vegetables became available, and the monthly harvest was over 8kg (18lb). During July, this one bed gave 21kg (46lb) of vegetables.

The quality of roots was mixed, because the manure, although well decomposed, needed more time to settle and become soil-like. Carrots forked a little but made a fair harvest, as did the beetroot. Onions were superb, with 72 bulbs weighing an average 140g (5oz) each, a nice medium size, all from just 14

Lettuce harvested weekly, and leeks establishing.

module plants, 7 of each variety. I pulled them in early August, left them in their rows for 10 days to dry in the occasional sun, then brought them into the greenhouse on trays.

The best-yielding vegetables in both the early and later parts of the year were the salad leaves – lettuce and endive respectively (see tables on page 188 and opposite), which fill plates on a regular basis. From one planting of lettuce I picked leaves for 4 months, and the planting of 14 endives gave leaves for all 3 months of autumn, taken by twisting off the lower leaves. The lettuce were a mixture of varieties, while the endives were frisée and scarole (see Chapter 7, page 115). Endive must be sown in summer only, because the plants flower in spring if sown early.

Clearing soil after the last harvest from each row

This is a quick job, because when you harvest with a second bucket to take debris such as potato leaves and rejects, there is almost nothing to clear after the final pick. In this bed it was just a case of twisting out stems of spinach, coriander, dill, lettuce and cabbage, cutting broad beans at soil level to leave their nitrogen nodules behind, and pulling out the odd weed.

Second crops

All the second-crop vegetables were sown in modules and grown under cover for a month, to be ready for planting as soon as space was clear after the first harvests. Some of them were interplanted between vegetables which were still growing.

Summer plantings of fennel, celery and endives.

Second crops in the bed							
Vegetable	Sown	Planted	Number of plants	Harvest	Yield		Notes
					kg	lb/oz	
French bean 'La Victoire'	Jun	Jul	5	Aug–Oct	1.74	3lb 14oz	Fast to crop
Beetroot 'Boltardy'	May	Jun	24	Aug–Nov	4.66	10lb 4oz	Rapid growth
Celery 'Tall Utah'	May	Jul	9	Oct–Nov	3.35	7lb 6oz	Slug damage
Swede 'Friese Gele'	May	Jun	6	Oct–Dec	7.92	17lb 7oz	Large roots
Leek 'Zermatt'	Apr	May	10	Oct–Nov	4.28	9lb 7oz	Tall stems
Endive 'Bubikopf', 'Fine Maraichere'	Jul	Aug	14	Sep–Nov	6.22	13lb 12oz	Outer leaves only, weekly
Florence fennel 'Montebianco'	Jul	Jul	5	Oct–Nov	0.92	2lb	6 nice bulbs
Kale 'Redbor', 'Cavolo Nero'	May	Jul	5	Sep–Dec	4.64	10lb 3oz	Redbor better
Cucumber 'La Diva'	May	Jun	1	Aug–Oct	3.29	7lb 4oz	20 fruits
Leek 'Bandit'	Apr	Jul	4	Oct–Dec	0.51	1lb 2oz	Moth damage

Interplanted vegetables

You can plant a successional crop between any growing vegetables that are either not giving total shade, or are soon to finish growing (see Chapter 11, page 172). My first interplant was in May, with module-grown small leek plants between lettuce. For 6 weeks the leeks barely grew, and looked pale from being outcompeted by the established lettuce plants, but they were putting roots down. By July, as the lettuce slowed down prior to flowering, the leek leaves became dark green and grew fast. If I had waited to plant them until after clearing the lettuce in high summer, the leeks would have needed to establish in the heat rather than being ready to grow well. Interplanting gains valuable time.

The beetroot grew fast, after I planted them 10cm (4") from large shallot plants on 25 June, as six modules of four plants in each. After the shallots were pulled on 6 July, the beets swelled so rapidly that I could harvest 1.2kg (2lb 10oz) on 15 August, with plenty more decent-sized roots through late summer and autumn.

The swedes were planted close to large and fast-growing shallots and lettuce, where they had just enough room to establish. By mid July, 3 weeks

October: all second plantings except parsnip at the far end.

after planting, they were well set with dark leaves, and had room to grow since the shallots and lettuce had finished. By autumn the swedes had grown large roots.

Weeding

After midsummer there are usually few annual weeds germinating in undisturbed soil and compost, and in this bed there was almost no weed growth at all, for three reasons. The first two are a basis of no-dig gardening; the third was a result of weather:

- Most weed seeds near the surface had already germinated and been hoed or removed.
- Perennial weeds including couch grass had almost exhausted the reserves of energy in their roots.
- The summer was dry, so new germinations were reduced.

Watering

Watering is most effective at planting time, with just small amounts needed to water new modules into the dry surface; then a few larger waterings are needed near harvest time, as leaves and beans are swelling, but only if the weather is dry. If unsure about watering, use a trowel to check moisture at deeper levels. A crumbly, dry surface serves as mulch for moisture below, and if you find that the soil is moist underneath, hold off from watering, as this will encourage plant roots to go deeper.

Harvests from second sowings

There was a nice spread of regular pickings over late summer and autumn, and from September to December the harvests averaged 10kg (22lb) each month. The first pick was of cucumbers from mid August: 'La Diva' is not the prettiest fruit, but is tasty and tender, as long as you pick every week at least, which involves hunting under the leaves.

Leaf vegetables such as endive and kale need picking regularly before they are too large and tough, or start to decay. Celery is best harvested before it is too large, and plants start to make new side-stems if you leave them too long.

Root vegetables give the most options for when you might harvest them; for example, swede and parsnip survive winter outdoors in the UK and can be harvested until early spring. I picked them by December because of needing to harvest at the same time as the adjacent experimental bed, which I dug before Christmas so that soil lumps could be broken by the winter frosts. This experience makes me appreciate the no-dig approach even more, because it is easier to overwinter vegetables without needing to do any soil-work.

The year's harvest of 85kg (187lb 6oz) from this bed reflects a year of good weather, many years' experience of growing, and a commitment to keep sowing and planting. It shows how small beds can be productive for many months.

Preparation for another year

After the last harvest of swede and kale in December, and pulling a few small weeds, I spread three wheelbarrow-loads of home-made compost on top of the clean surface. Just before that I planted broad beans and garlic. It took an hour, and the bed was now ready for the following seasons of sowing, planting and picking.

It is often said that the gardening new year begins in autumn or early winter, before the calendar new year, and this example illustrates the point well.

The bed on the right has simply been covered with compost.

CHAPTER THIRTEEN

Growing under cover

Harvests all year round

"He who sows peas on the highway does not get all the pods into his barn."

Danish proverb

Any structure providing cover to protect plants will increase growth potential. Whether made from glass or plastic, they enable earlier harvests in spring, exotic crops in summer, and growth of higher quality and yield through winter. This chapter considers the relative advantages of different types of structure, and explains the differences in technique when growing under cover rather than outdoors. It gives cultivation details for spring- and summer-sown crops, including some interesting and unusual vegetables, and winter salads too.

For a large covered structure, the main options are a greenhouse or a polytunnel. A conservatory is possible, but is more challenging to maintain as a suitable growing environment (see page 199).

Cost considerations

There is a substantial monetary difference between greenhouses and polytunnels, and as a result of making the comparisons outlined here, I now appreciate my polytunnel even more for its cost-effectiveness. However, I did choose an expensive greenhouse, and you can erect simpler aluminium ones from a kit. Previously I had made my own greenhouse from scratch, spending little on its reclaimed materials but investing much time. At Homeacres I had insufficient time to do this, and bought a wooden structure of red cedar, measuring 12x25' (3.6x7.5m) (greenhouses and polytunnels are generally sold in imperial dimensions).

Greenhouse

Greenhouses are solid structures and need a firm footing, usually of concrete, and for larger ones also a low wall. Wooden greenhouses look pretty but need more maintenance and exclude more light than aluminium greenhouses, whose framework is thinner.

My new greenhouse rising out of the February mud.

Mine cost a hefty £7,000, which included aluminium bars over the wooden rafters, a propagation table, extra side windows and erection by four men in half a day only. The greenhouse sits on top of a precisely measured 40cm (16") brick wall of two courses, built by my neighbour Mark for £2,400. Construction during a wet winter caused compaction of soil by a dumper truck and digger, but the finished greenhouse looks great in the garden.

Polytunnel

Polytunnels come in all sizes, heights and strength of hoops, and with different options for burying the polythene or securing it to wooden or metal strips along the ground. Burying the edges in soil is preferable, for two reasons:

- The polythene serves to anchor the whole structure in place during high wind, so there is no need for concrete to anchor the foundation tubes.
- Because the polythene goes down into soil, it serves as a barrier to exclude entry of weeds and pests.

My tunnel was second-hand, 12 years old. It measures 18x31' (5.5x9.5m) and has semicircular hoops. Newer tunnels have hoops with 1m (3') vertical sides, which are good for growing taller plants in the side beds and for positioning a propagating bench along any side. They also make it easier to harvest plants near the edges.

A new price for my tunnel is around £1,000, but all I needed was a new sheet of polythene for £150, and some wood and screws for the door frames for £50, which just shows how economical polytunnels are. Robin helped with dismantling and moving it from its old site, then Steph helped with putting up the hoops at Homeacres, and we were joined by her son Ruairi on an excitingly breezy January day for the covering. We managed to pull the polythene over and quickly buried its side into pre-dug trenches, whose soil contained bits of concrete, tree roots and roots of dandelion, cow parsley and couch grass. But the soil was crumbly and dark and promised well.

Tip: When putting up a polytunnel, lay some cardboard along the edges and into the trench, to slow down weeds pushing up from the edges, which are otherwise difficult to keep clean (see photo overleaf, top left). Covering is easier in warm sunshine, when the polythene is softer and you can pull it tighter when burying its edge and attaching it to the frame.

1. January: trenches dug and cardboard mulch along edges. 2. Spreading compost mulch.
3. Less rotted manure for the paths, and cardboard all over. 4. A final mulch of finer compost.

Growth and harvests in different structures

It is fascinating to see how growth of the same plants varies in different structures. Light levels, light quality, ventilation, humidity and heat retention are all different, with some plants affected more than others.

Greenhouse

A visiting nurseryman suggested that there was too little ventilation in my greenhouse, because the equivalent of 20 per cent of the floor area should be openable for air, whereas mine has only 15 per cent openable, with the internal temperature in high summer sometimes exceeding 45°C (113°F) in the afternoon. Three of the fourteen tomato plants lost their growing points and suffered blossom end rot from an irregular uptake of water.

On the other hand, cucumbers and melons grew well, and three 'Black Pearl' F1 aubergine plants gave a phenomenal harvest, helped by the hot summer.

Then during winter there was a striking difference in leaf colour and quality of plants in my greenhouse and polytunnel (see page 213): the leaves of many salads were paler and thinner in the greenhouse, due to reduced light levels caused by the sturdy wooden struts in its roof.

Polytunnel

Growth in the polytunnel was generally a little stronger, helped by the polythene's light-diffusing quality. It allows 89 per cent of light through, including ultraviolet (UV), which promotes good leaf

July, and cucumbers are growing 5cm (2") per day.

colour, although the plastic is not the more expensive heat-retentive ('thermic') or anti-condensation grade. All the plants I have grown in the polytunnel have done well, and even though it is a little cooler than the greenhouse by night, many harvests have been higher in the end thanks to the better light levels, and airflow too.

A strong point of polytunnels is ventilation, with the openings at both ends allowing an airflow on even the hottest days, as warm air rises out of both doorways. However, in longer structures there can be pockets of 'dead air' in the middle. To allow passage of fresh air all the time, I left a gap above the door panels, at a height of 2m (6'6"): winter salads crop well in this small airflow, with the doors themselves closed much of the time. It is more important to have some ventilation, to reduce fungal diseases, than to try to keep all warmth in.

Conservatory

It is more difficult to grow plants successfully in a conservatory, as either type of roof has its problems. A glass roof lets more light in but causes extreme temperatures, since, unlike in a greenhouse, the roof panels themselves are not openable. A tiled roof, on the other hand, keeps warmth in during winter and reduces heat in summer, but allows in too little light for strong growth. You also need to take more care when watering, to avoid mess. That said, it is possible to raise reasonable plants on a conservatory windowsill.

I use the wide window ledge of my conservatory in autumn to finish ripening peppers and chillies on pot-grown plants, and to over-winter plants such as stevia and chillies. The sunny window ledge is also ideal for ripening winter squash, drying beans and seeds, and chitting potatoes.

December: a habanero chilli in the conservatory.

Weeds and watering

When excavating soil for concrete footings to build the greenhouse wall on, Mark pointed out that all the turves were full of couch grass roots. I was worried and decided to mulch inside to a thickness of 20cm (8") – thicker than the 15cm (6") mulch I used in the tunnel. I also laid overlapping, thick cardboard in both structures.

As a result, couch grass regrowth was minimal, and Mark – once a farmer and knowing the difficulty of coping with it – was subsequently impressed. Some bindweed appeared, mostly from late summer onwards, but the mulch was so effective that I spent almost no time weeding in the greenhouse.

In the polytunnel we used trowels to remove some re-growing dandelions and buttercups in spring, and I covered one area of persisting couch grass with black polythene in April, before planting melons through it. Summer weeding was little and often, mainly of bindweed on one side, which by October was the only remaining perennial weed. Annual weeds in the surface compost were few and far between, easy to pull whenever I saw a new weed seedling.

1 & 2. Spreading a deep mulch of compost before and after erection of the greenhouse. **3.** Beds ready. **4.** May: plantings through biodegradable polythene; plants being raised in modules on the right.

Germination of new weeds

Under cover you have more control of annual weed growth than outdoors: you simply reduce germination by watering thoroughly and less frequently. Keeping the surface mainly dry resulted in there being almost no annual weeds in both greenhouse and polytunnel. Any that did emerge were easy to hoe, dislodge or pull out of the compost mulch when small.

Watering

Watering by hand is sometimes seen as a waste of time, compared with using automatic devices. However, while watering you also do a lot of gardening by having a good look, noticing plants that need care and weeds to remove. In addition, hand watering is more sensitive to the needs of each plant: you can give more to those in full growth; less to small plants and when fruiting vegetables such as tomatoes, peppers and chillies need to ripen in autumn.

I water with a hose from water butts if it has rained enough. Using watering cans is hard graft and takes time, but keeps you fit. When the butts are nearly empty I brush around the inside and tip them to rinse out the debris, so that the water is sweet.

Organic matter holds moisture, therefore with a decent layer of mulch you can water less often and with a good dose each time, especially if you have heavy soil.

Watering basil in July.

Look for the surface to dry thoroughly between each watering, in order to reduce weeds, fungal disease and slug movements around plants.

The polytunnel and greenhouse are similar in their moisture requirements: I water every 3 or 4 days on average through the summer, but every 2 days in any intense heat. During winter, after saturating the soil before planting winter vegetables, I water every fortnight on average; less if cold, or weekly if mild.

Spring vegetables under cover

Covered structures have two benefits: they enlarge the repertoire of plants you can grow, and extend the seasons in which plants can grow. This section offers ideas for extending the season of spring-sown vegetables, to have earlier harvests of crops that you can also grow outside. According to when they finish cropping, you can then plant warmth-loving crops such as basil, melon and cape gooseberry, as well as salads and other vegetables. (All spacings are either one measurement, equidistant between plants, or two measurements, between plants and rows – see box in Chapter 10, page 155.)

Peas for shoots

Spacing: 30cm (12")
Sow two peas per module on a windowsill in mid winter, and plant them a month later, for pea shoots to pick throughout spring. Yield is high if you use a tall variety, and weekly or twice-weekly picking of all new shoots keeps plants immature and making new growth.

Peas for pods

Spacing: 15x45cm (6x18")
You can sow peas in late autumn: module sowing is good, compared with direct sowing, when mice often find the pea seeds. I set some November-sown plants into the polytunnel's surface compost on a snowy day in January. 'Feltham First' cropped in early spring, then 'Kelvedon Wonder' a week later. Early peas are a great treat.

Broad beans

Spacing: 15x45cm (6x18")
Broad beans overwinter outside in milder areas, but in cold winters it can be worth growing a few under cover. My November-sown 'Aquadulce', planted in January in the polytunnel, took ages to start growing but eventually cropped 3 weeks ahead of outdoor plants.

Beetroot

Spacing: 30-40cm (12-16") in module-sown clumps
'Boltardy' beetroot, sown four seeds to a module in late winter and raised under cover, can be planted in early spring as clumps, with an average of four seedlings together. Beetroot thrive in spring light, and roots can quickly reach tennis-ball size – mine were ready by early May.

Courgette

Spacing: 60cm (24")
Sow in early spring and plant after 3 weeks, once the main frost season is past, to harvest from late May. Courgette plants grow big, and by solstice

time they are gobbling up lots of precious protected space, and need plenty of water. After picking for 1 month only, by which time outdoor courgettes are producing, you may want to remove them and plant something more space-efficient, for example basil.

Sweetcorn

Spacing: 30cm (12")
Sow in early April in modules, for planting 4 weeks later. I grew 'Sweet Nugget' F1 and they gave two sweet cobs per plant in the last week of July. I was keen to harvest them before the possible arrival of badgers, who can smash holes in polytunnel plastic. Luckily they did not!

Summer vegetables under cover

The plants in this section benefit from the extra warmth of growing under cover, and they can be so productive that summer gluts are quite likely. Do follow the advice given here on spacing, because the large size of these vegetables means that too close a planting can lead to diseases, as well as cause difficulties in harvesting.

These crops grow fast and need constant care. One way of saving time is to give no feeds to soil-grown plants, as all the food they need can be provided by a mulch of compost on top and undisturbed soil below. For plants in containers and growbags, feeding is necessary from midsummer.

Tomato

Spacing: 45-50cm (18-20")
Sow seed in modules, and a month later put these into 7cm (3") pots, probably re-potting once before planting in the first half of May. For planting indeterminate cordon varieties (the ones that need side shoots removing and grow tall) in soil, put a knotted end of string under the rootball at planting time. This will be held in place by developing roots. Tie the other end to supporting wires above head level, and the stems will twist around it as they grow. You can use the same method for cucumbers – it is so quick and easy.

Indoor tomatoes need continual training, pruning, picking and careful watering. From midsummer, when spores of late blight are prevalent, you can keep tomatoes healthy by watering only the soil and compost, so that their leaves are dry and blight spores have no wet leaves to develop on. To ensure that all fruits ripen before winter, pinch out the main growing points in late summer and all subsequent side shoots, so that plants are nourishing only existing trusses, which then have time to mature before frost.

Reduce watering in late summer; after mid September you need scarcely water at all, so that plants' energy is diverted from new growth to ripening existing fruit, with concentration of flavours and sweetness. Keep removing all side shoots, and cut off leaves below the lowest truss with fruit on. This allows you to

October: the last 'Yellow Brandywine', and new salads.

water the soil without wetting the leaves. Retain all leaves above the lowest truss, for continuing photosynthesis to allow fruit growth and a full flavour.

There are many varieties to choose from: I recommend 'Sungold' (orange cherry tomato), for being fast to crop and of great flavour. Beef tomatoes come in an exciting range of sizes and colours; they ripen a little later and often give a glut in late summer.

Melon

Spacing: 60cm (24")
Melons need a warm summer to fruit well, even under cover. There are many good varieties for a temperate climate and, after potting on twice, you can have large plants to set out in early summer. Either grow them up strings, as for tomatoes (see opposite), or on the ground, in which case you need to pinch out growing tips once fruits are half-size, every few days. Water little when melons are full-size,

August, and 'Sweetheart' melons are ripe.

though be aware that their roots will travel a long way to pinch water from other plants!

They can give four to six melons per plant, often ripening all together and within a fortnight in late summer. Outdoor plantings or cool summers result in later ripening with a less intense flavour and sweetness.

Cucumber

Spacing: 60cm (24")
Don't sow too early: mid spring is fine, as it's then easier to keep plants as warm as possible until planting 1 month after sowing. Remove the first two or three tiny cucumbers to make for stronger harvests from plants that are well established. In any hot weather cucumbers crop prolifically, and need watering every 2 days when growing in soil; every day or twice a day in containers.

Aubergine

Spacing: 50cm (20")
Aubergines need heat to produce well, and really benefit from being under cover in temperate climates. For large fruits, 'Black Pearl' F1 is a winner, or 'Moneymaker' for a non-hybrid. Aubergine plants need almost as much water as tomatoes but less maintenance, just occasional removal of yellow leaves, and tying loosely to a central supporting stake.

Aubergine 'Black Pearl' F1 in September.

Pepper

Spacing: 45-50cm (18-20")
Grow sweet peppers like aubergines and with similar maintenance, just a little less water, for a few green peppers by the middle of summer. Temperate climates are marginal for achieving big harvests of sweet coloured peppers, whose main season is autumn, as they need plenty of warmth and 2-4 weeks to ripen on the plant.

Chilli pepper

Spacing: 45-50cm (18-20")
These are similar to sweet peppers for needing most of summer and autumn to mature and ripen: they are prolific, so one or two plants should be enough, in soil or 30cm (12") pots. Also, they are feasible to grow as perennials if you have a light, frost-free place for them in winter. For example, my two jalapeño plants had 24 chillies each, with many ripe by mid autumn, when I brought the plants into the conservatory. By Christmas their fruits were all red, and we continued picking fresh chillies until March. Then I cut them back to woody stems, re-potted with fresh compost, and put them back in the polytunnel to grow again.

Basil

Spacing: 40-45cm (16-18")
This herb is the perfect complement to tomato, and so rewarding that it deserves space in any greenhouse or polytunnel. The many flavours include lime and lemon varieties, or if you want maximum harvests grow Genovese sweet basil.

Sow mid spring in warmth in seed trays or modules, plant about 6 weeks later, and pick weekly from early summer. Here are some tips for a long season of abundant basil:

Basil is healthy under cover.

- Plants need room to grow, and do well at the spacings given here, with a mulch of compost around them, or just one plant in a 25cm (10") pot of compost.

- Pick at least weekly – all new shoots and a few larger leaves – and sweet basil can give 60g (2oz) per plant per week in high summer.
- Keep plants tidy by removing flower stalks and any yellowing leaves.
- Water twice weekly and thoroughly, on the soil only unless it is hot, as basil leaves risk browning from lying wet in cool and cloudy weather.

Some unusual vegetables

The vegetables covered in this section are mostly new to UK gardeners, and those who have tried them so far have often had mixed results. Some are worth growing at least once, for an appreciation of what is worth giving precious space to, and I share my experiences of them to help clarify some advantages and disadvantages.

Sweet potato
(*Ipomoea batatas*)

Spacing: 60cm (24")
Mine grew mixed harvests, from plants of three varieties which Steph had raised from slips, which are shoots from last season's tubers, rather like the chits on potatoes. I set them out in early summer and harvested in mid autumn. The feeble-looking outdoor plant in a 25cm (10") pot by the shed's south side, variety 'Beauregard', had two decent-sized tubers of 330g (12oz). But the greenhouse plant, variety 'T65', which had trailed healthily in all directions and needed some pruning, had no tubers at all! My sanity was restored by the polytunnel plant of 'Carolina Ruby', which yielded 2.6kg (5lb 12oz) of large roots, which I put to sweeten in a carrier bag in the warm conservatory, because the flavour is poor if you eat them when just harvested.

Carolina Ruby was also the only variety to offer pretty flowers, every day from July to October, similar to and smaller than morning glory (*Ipomoea purpurea*): both are in the Convolvulaceae family, along with bindweeds. Hence their rapid growth when given enough warmth, but outdoor growing of sweet potato is marginal in most of the UK.

Oca / New Zealand yam
(*Oxalis tuberosa*)

Spacing: 45cm (18")
Oca has potential: the plants are healthy, yields are fair, the roots are pretty

and flavoursome (both raw and cooked) and easy to store and replant, and the clover-like leaves are tasty in salad. I grew three plants in the polytunnel and two outside, set out in late spring after the last frost. I found watering hard to judge, as the leaves can look a little shrivelled, and under-watered the polytunnel plants, whose harvest of 1.4kg was poor compared with 2.2kg outdoors (3lb 1oz and 4lb 14oz respectively), so it would seem that under-cover growing is not worthwhile in this climate.

Do not harvest oca too early, because they need a frost to kill leaves and help roots to finish swelling in autumn. The brightly coloured tubers are clustered and easy to gather: rinse them at harvest time and set in sunshine on a windowsill, to improve the flavour. They are different from potatoes, with no blight issues or risk of harm from light on the tubers. The plants like a spadeful of compost sprinkled over the developing crown in July, as both plant food and for tubers to swell in.

Cape gooseberry
(*Physalis peruviana*)

Spacing: 45cm (18")
These fruits need a decent period of warmth to mature golden-yellow, with enough sweetness to balance the strong acidity. Sow in early spring on a heated bed, plant early summer, and harvest from late summer until frost. When I grew them I encountered three drawbacks:

- The plants are vigorous and hard to prune, rapidly making new shoots from all of the many original branch ends, so they can overshadow nearby plants. Also, despite plenty of staking, tying in and trimming, there are often stems and fruit on the soil.
- Ripening occurs randomly at all levels, so the yellowing fruits hide or fall in

Cape gooseberry in September.

unsuspected places, difficult to gather without knocking off nearby green ones. One method is to shake the plants and gather fallen fruits.

- Few of my customers were impressed by the flavour. I like it, and if you do, I suggest growing a smaller, patio variety: on the patio works well if it is sheltered and sunny. Use a 25cm (10") pot, as they are hungry and thirsty plants, even the small ones.

Stevia
(*Stevia rebaudiana*)

Spacing: 35-40cm (14-16")
These elegant plants have remarkable leaves, many times sweeter than sugar but with a different kind of sweetness – slower to activate on the tongue and giving a liquorice aftertaste, not to everybody's liking. They work well in smoothies, muffins and for sweetening rhubarb.

Sow in early spring in warmth, for setting out after last frost, as plants grow slowly at first. Two months later you can be picking some of the larger leaves. More pickings follow until mid October. Then prune hard and dig out the main rootball, to pot on and keep growing in a frost-free place. Replant these in late spring.

After each harvest, you can put leaves in a dehydrator for three hours at 40°C (104°F), or in bright sunshine, until they are crackling dry. Then crumble them to a green dust of ultra-sweet flavour, easy to store in a jam jar.

Cucamelon
(*Melothria scabra*)

Spacing: 60cm (24")
These are rampant plants that fruit at all levels, making it difficult to find all the ripe ones. The fruits are of average flavour and with little resemblance to melon, so I was disappointed to have given the plants valuable space. Another name for this fruit is 'Mexican sour gherkin', and this is a more accurate description than 'cucamelon'.

Bitter gourd (or bitter melon)
(*Momordica charantia*)

Spacing: 75cm (30")
These need much heat to succeed, and I was pleased to pass the first test of germination, from a sowing in early summer, after which early growth in modules and small pots was rapid. I planted one in the greenhouse and four in the tunnel (two gourd, two melon), after removing pea plants in

late June. They grew rapidly in the heat of high summer, racing up strings at 7cm (3") a day, until they were taller than me. But for all that, in both greenhouse and tunnel, there were just four flowers and one immature, wizened fruit. This temperate climate is just not hot enough for them.

September sowings for winter salads

Wonderful summer vegetables are only half the story. An amazing range of salad leaves can be grown under cover through the darker and cooler half of the year, at a time when many other vegetables are growing little. It works well to sow into modules in early autumn, when tomatoes and other summer plants are still cropping. Throughout autumn you need to pull these plants out immediately after final harvests, and pop in the mix of your salad plants in October, with many flavours to choose from – see table below. The salads are listed in suggested order of sowing date.

Winter salads under cover, for planting in October				
Salad plant	Sow	First pick	Last pick	Qualities
Parsley	Aug	Oct–Nov	May	Rich flavours
Wild rocket	Aug	Oct–Nov	Jun-Jul	Spicy, good in spring
Land cress	Aug	Oct–Nov	May	Pepper flavour
Sorrel (broad & buckler)	Aug	Nov	Jul	Lemon flavours
Spinach	Early Sep	Nov	Jun	Many sweet leaves
Ruby chard	Early Sep	Nov	May	Great colour, space at 10cm (4")*
Lettuce 'Grenoble Red'	Early Sep	Nov	Jun	Hardy, abundant, long lived
Chervil / dill / coriander	Early Sep	Nov	May	Top flavours
Endive (frisée & scarole)	Mid Sep	Nov	Early May	Abundant
Winter purslane	Mid Sep	Nov	Late Apr	Mild taste, flowers in April
Pak choi	Mid Sep	Nov	Apr	Mild, crunchy stems
Mustards (many kinds)	Mid Sep	Nov	Early May	Great colours & tastes
Salad rocket	Mid Sep	Nov	Early May	Peppery
Leaf radish	Late Sep	Nov	Late Apr	Large, radish flavour
Mizuna	Late Sep	Nov	Late Apr	Many mild leaves

*See overleaf.

Salad plants in December, to crop until April.

Spacing is related to picking

For both simplicity and ease of harvesting leaves, I use the same spacing for almost all salad plants: 22-25cm (9-10"). This allows each plant ample room for an extensive root run, so that it continues producing healthy leaves for up to 6 months. Chard is an exception, as it can quickly grow large, so small, immature leaves for salad are best grown at a closer spacing. For most plants listed in the table, you plant once and pick 20 times. Once everything is in the ground by mid autumn, the main job until spring is regular harvesting of outer leaves, with occasional watering and weeding.

Ground preparation and watering

This is the sequence of events before planting:
- Gently pull out stems of summer plants, cutting off most of their roots in the process, leaving all smaller roots in the soil.
- Remove all weeds (and there should be very few, because of your regular weeding and infrequent summer waterings, therefore minimal germination of weed seeds).
- Walk on the surface to firm it back down and break any larger lumps, making it level. This causes no compaction, because of the soil having compost on top and being quite dry.
- Water until fully moist, which often means watering a little every day, since dry compost and soil need time to absorb water again – if you try to water all at once, some of it runs off or through and down. I find this especially after tomatoes, which continue to draw moisture from deeper

down when being watered less in early autumn (see page 205). When you have spread compost in spring, before planting summer vegetables, there should be no need to add more in autumn: the soil should still be fertile enough for winter vegetables.

Winter and spring harvests

Pickings through late autumn are usually followed by a lull when it turns cold and the days are at their shortest, with only a few small leaves to harvest. Keep plants tidy at this time by removing yellow or diseased leaves, together with any weeds and slugs, and water sparingly if at all.

As light levels increase rapidly from late winter, and temperatures too, you notice leaves improve in quality – becoming larger, thicker, glossier and also more numerous with every passing week, until by mid spring there can be a major abundance, until plants start to make flowering stems. Many of the first flower buds and stems are good to eat, until the stems become more woody, and the flowers of winter purslane are a feast for the eye as well. Once plants are making more stem than salad, I twist them out and spread 5cm (2") of compost, to have soil ready for planting summer vegetables from late spring.

Growth in the greenhouse and the polytunnel

My winter salad plants grew abundantly in their first year in both the greenhouse and the polytunnel, but there were two interesting differences, which must have been related to the greenhouse being made of wood:

- Stronger colours on leaves in the polytunnel, as a result of higher light levels. Leaves on the same plants in the greenhouse were paler and thinner.
- Longer cropping of poly-tunnel plants, probably also related to the light difference, and perhaps also to more spring warmth in the greenhouse, where flowering stems appeared a week earlier on average.

So the greenhouse salads looked a little less impressive, although they were perfectly healthy and productive.

Outdoor-grown (left) and greenhouse-grown (right) lettuce.

CHAPTER FOURTEEN

Hot beds

Using the heat of fresh manure to extend the season

"As the garden grows, so does the gardener."

Anon.

This chapter is for you if you have a liking to try something different. You need access to fresh manure, and enough time and muscle power to assemble it into a heap, with a growing bed on top, then to disassemble it all in autumn, before starting again in late winter. If you're prepared to make the investment, hot beds are an exciting way of starting the season early, and with abundant summer growth too. Here I explain how to make a hot bed, and describe the results of my first year's growing on two different outdoor hot beds. More detailed information can be found in Jack First's book *Hot Beds* (see Resources).

The hot bed season

Hot beds make possible the seemingly impossible, above all in late winter and spring. This time is when the air is cold but the days are bright and lengthening: therefore the heat from a heap of fresh manure gives plants enough warmth to use the light and grow, when they would otherwise stay mostly dormant. My beds amaze visitors with their harvestable beetroot, carrot, lettuce, radish and spinach, during cool spring weather when most of the garden has only seedlings.

Timings for best value

I have made outdoor hot beds at two main times of year, in mid and late winter. Both have worked, to varying degrees, and I have found that in higher latitudes (Homeacres is 51°N) late winter is the best season to assemble them for early sowings and harvests. If made earlier, the main heat is produced when there is too little light for plants to use it effectively. If made later, on the other hand, hot beds would give less return for all the effort involved, by comparison with plants growing faster in ordinary soil as it warms up in spring.

The value of produce from hot beds is relative to the weather in spring. For example, the cold spring of 2013 gave extra value to my later hot bed, which produced long before other outdoor beds, while in a warm spring it would have been less advantageous.

If you make just one hot bed, I suggest making it in early to mid February for milder areas (equivalent to zone 9), and late February in cooler areas

This new hot bed has just been sown.

(zone 8) where frost is usually prevalent in March and even in April. Whichever date you start, there is the added bonus of residual warmth and plenty of fertility for second plantings in early summer (see page 227).

The base

A hot bed for vegetable growing is actually two beds: one a base of fresh organic matter, decomposing and giving out heat (the actual 'hot bed'); the other a smaller bed on top, of mature compost. The first step is to create the 'engine room' below.

Heat intensity and duration

The heat output of the bed is influenced by both the heap size and the ingredients used. In essence:

- Large heaps grow hotter and their heat lasts longer. A width of 1.2-1.5m (4-5') is good for the bottom bed, so the middle of the top bed will be reachable. You can go for as much length as you like.
- The depth of manure, after trampling to consolidate it, wants to be at least 45cm (18") and preferably more, for the same reason. Avoid depths over 75cm (30"), unless expecting frosty weather over the coming few weeks (see page 222).
- Fresh manure has more potential energy than 3- or 4-week-old manure, and horse manure heats more strongly than cow or most other animals' manure.

February: filling a pallet enclosure with horse manure.

- The animals' bedding material makes a difference; for example, straw heats more quickly than wood shavings, but the gentler heat of wood lasts for longer.

Assembling the hot bed

If using horse manure with straw bedding, a heap can stand without sides, held together by the long pieces of straw. Always build the sides before the centre, really packing manure along all edges, and trampling it, before filling the middle, in order to keep it level.

Heap filled to maximum; needs levelling and trampling.

Alternatively, you can create wooden sides, but this adds expense and can also make picking difficult, as you have to lean over the side to tend a growing bed that is dropping all the time, as the manure decreases in volume. If using manure with wood shavings, it will need to be contained in an enclosure.

Even with an enclosure for the base ingredients, it is still good to do some trampling on the manure and bedding while filling, to squash as much as possible into whatever space you have, especially the edges and corners. Otherwise your heap will sink too quickly, also unevenly, and produce less heat. Again, you need to make it level before placing the growing bed on top.

The growing bed

A hot bed is no good for growing plants itself, since its ingredients are not decomposed. You need a growing bed on top, for sowing and planting into. Later on, as spring turns to summer, vegetables can send roots into the maturing manure below, for both nutrients and moisture.

Frame on top filled with compost, which is in contact with the fresh manure.

Framework

To contain the compost for the growing bed, wooden planks 15cm (6")
wide and 3-5cm (1-2") thick can be screwed together using metal corner
braces, or screwed to corner posts of 5x5cm (2x2"). You can make them
on the ground and then lift the whole frame into place, or assemble them
in situ: frames sit on top of the fresh manure, with no securing needed.

Size-wise, it is good for the sides and ends of the growing bed to be
15-30cm (6-12") shorter than the base bed, in order that:

- the compost in the growing bed is well supported at the edges,
  whereas it might run down and out if the edge of this bed were too
  close to the edge of the hot bed
- you can pack some fresh manure around the growing bed's sides and
  ends, as insulation (see photos on page 223).

Ingredients and filling

The materials for the growing bed are similar to those used in a normal
bed, namely any compost that is dark and crumbly. A 15cm (6") depth of
compost is good, tamped down with a spade as you fill it, to avoid air holes.
My first bed was filled entirely with home-made compost from the previous
spring, then my second bed contained a mix of green-waste compost and
home-made compost, with some 18-month-old cow and horse manure as
well. Growth was good in both beds, but better in the first one.

Unlike when making normal beds, there is no time for the top bed's
surface compost to weather and become fine, because you need to get

Early March, and the hot bed is planted and covered with a fleece cloche.

seeds and plants in as soon as possible after the bed is filled, to make the most of early and intense heat. Therefore you need to keep your finest compost for the top 3cm (1") or so, to make sowing and planting easier.

Covering

Beds need a cover to contain the warmth around plants, otherwise it is blown away by cold winds and only the plants' roots are warmed. One option is 'lights', which are wooden frames covered by polythene or glass, as with a cold frame; another is fleece over cloche hoops.

For my first bed I made two large frames out of 5x3cm (2x1") battens, over which I stretched UV-resistant polythene, secured with thin strips of wood along the inside edges. These covers are 2x1.7m (80x68"), and I soon realized that they are too cumbersome for one person to lift. Also, they are vulnerable to high winds, and I had to screw them down for a while, which made it slower to remove them for watering, weeding and harvesting.

For the second bed I created a simpler, quicker cover of 2m (80")-wide fleece, suspended over wire hoops and held in place by stones or wood along the sides and ends. Although fleece holds less heat than polythene covers, it keeps the cold wind out, warms up nicely in any sunshine, and is easy to push back for access to plants.

Sowing and planting

Early sowings are in non-ideal conditions: my first one was during light snowfall, and it was difficult to draw drills in the wet, sticky compost.

Problems

These may not affect you, but the three main potential problems are black-birds, moles and manure contaminants.

These beds contain many worms, and local wildlife may get interested! I found that blackbirds kick out a lot of the hot beds' edges as they seek its worms, and they can also make a mess of the growing bed once the covers are removed in fine weather. Covering the whole set-up with bird netting is the main remedy, but it slows access for picking, planting and weeding.

Jack First, who pioneered this version of outdoor hot beds in Yorkshire, had problems with moles eating worms in the hot bed, and that slowed its decomposition. If you already have moles in` the garden, perhaps a hot bed is not a good idea unless you employ a trapper.

The weedkiller aminopyralid is a possible, if unlikely, problem: it should not be present, because horse hay made from grass on which it has been sprayed is not supposed to be sold. So it should detectable by simply asking horse owners whether they use their own hay, and if so, whether it was made from grass that had been sprayed with this lethal poison. However, things never work out so smoothly, and even after taking these precautions I have had problems in my second year at Homeacres. The best way to avoid this is to find manure from someone who makes his or her own hay without using this poison, and in whom you feel confident.

However, although the drills were less smooth than usual, the seeds germinated well. I filled the drills after sowing with 1cm (½") of fine potting compost.

For later beds you can set out some January-sown plants in addition to seed, which speeds up the whole process. I was able to compare plantings of lettuce, spinach, peas, beetroot and spring onion in late February, with direct sowings of the same vegetables in January: they all grew well, with the best harvests from planting rather than from sowing, with the exception of carrots.

First sowings and harvests

It was a good spring for seeing the benefits of hot beds, with 27 frosts between 1 March and 7 April, and plenty of cold winds. Hot beds are more exposed to wind than beds at ground level, so the lights and fleece are needed by plants, and allow more use of the warmth before it disperses or is blown away.

Weather context

The table below shows the weather at Homeacres in the first part of the year when I made my hot beds, giving a background to the growing results on the following pages. Apart from in January, temperatures and rainfall were below average, with cool, dry winds.

The weather at Homeacres during the hot bed season		Jan	Feb	Mar	Apr	May	Jun
Average high temperature	°C	7.1	6.2	7.9	12.5	14.9	19.6
	°F	44.8	43.2	46.2	54.5	58.8	67.3
Average low temperature	°C	1.9	0.3	-0.1	2.9	4.9	10.0
	°F	35.4	32.5	31.8	37.2	40.8	50.0
Rain	mm	97	37	47	32	60	33
	inches	3⁷/₈	1¹/₂	1⁷/₈	1¹/₄	2³/₈	1¹/₄
Sunshine hours		58	59	86	147	172	173
Number of frosts		14	14	20	10	1	0

By comparison, the following spring was far milder, so the hot beds gave less benefit compared with ordinary beds, which started cropping sooner. Also, I found that in a warm spring, a deep hot bed of 1m (40") manure was too hot, causing some damage to roots in the warmer middle of the growing bed, while plants on the edges grew well.

Therefore I suggest a depth of 60-75cm (24-30") fresh manure in areas with mild springs, but if you have snow and frost in March, a deeper base is worthwhile. In this case, leave it a week after assembly and before sowing, to shed the greater, initial heat.

Hot bed 1

Growing bed: 1.4x3m (4'6"x9'10"), made with 25cm (10") planks.
The base had a 60cm (24") starting depth of fresh manure. With hindsight, this worked well in every way, although it seemed a little 'cool' at the time. The shallower hot bed meant a little more air in the manure than there would otherwise have been, and it decomposed to make better compost.

The wooden sides above the level of base manure had some gaps between the planks, so even when the covers were on, there was sufficient ventilation.

Sowings and growing

I sowed the whole bed on 21 January, then kept covers on for a month, until I needed to do some light weeding and thin the newly emerged seedlings. Spacings were 18cm (7") between rows and 10cm (4") between plants, after thinning, except for carrots and onions at 2-3cm (1"). This spacing between rows is closer than is usual in a bed, making it necessary to keep picking leaves and roots when small, before they overshadow their neighbours.

Most seedlings were visible after 3 weeks, with slow but steady growth thereafter. I removed the covers every week to water, or watered after picking, and slug damage was slight – helped by a toad lurking under a plank on the outer manure.

The results were variable. The following is an account of these crops, row by row: I list the failures as well as the successes here, to give you an idea of what is worth sowing.

- Spinach 'Boa' F1: large leaves from early April to June.
- Carrot 'Early Milan Nantes' and some parsley, both flat-leaved and curly: thinnings in April; cropped May and June. The Nantes carrots had great flavour.
- Lettuce 'Diveria', 'Freckles', 'Delicato': red/speckled outer leaves from April to mid July, but Delicato flowered in June.
- Carrot 'Amsterdam Forcing': long, thin roots through May, early June.
- Lettuce 'Claremont': green cos leaves from late April until 19 July.
- Carrot 'Early Nantes': for all the carrots I used thinnings as small, early harvests, to allow the remaining roots to grow large. They were easy to pull out of the compost and did not fork.

From March (left) to April (right) growth is rapid.

- Spinach 'Toscane': poor growth from old seed, so I interplanted 'Boa' on 8 March and picked as for the first row.
- Carrot 'Amsterdam Forcing'.
- Beetroot 'Boltardy', 'Bull's Blood': slow from old seed, then I interplanted more Boltardy on 8 March and took harvests from mid May – the first roots of golf-ball size and wonderful, sweet flavour.
- Onion 'Red Baron' and 'Mammoth' for plants to go in the main garden (half-rows): Mammoth poor germination and I pulled them all to eat in May. The red onions were pretty in salad; I did not need them as plants after all.
- Beetroot 'Boltardy'.
- Onion 'North Holland Blood Red' and shallot 'Conservor' F1 for plants (half-rows): again I had enough plants from greenhouse-sown modules, so pulled these in May for salads.
- Beetroot 'Boltardy'.
- Coriander 'Filtro': excellent vigour and welcome flavour; picked from mid April until flowering in mid June.
- Pea 'Kelvedon Wonder': first flowers on 10 May and good pickings throughout June, from 90cm (36") plants supported on hazel sticks. The supports reduced overshadowing of the coriander and brassicas nearby.
- Cabbage 'Greyhound' and dill 'Domino' (half-rows): dill slow and small pickings; cabbage harvested as small plants for salad greens in April and May. Not enough space for hearting cabbage.
- Calabrese 'Chevalier' F1: again, harvested as young plants for salad leaves, then I wished I had left three or four to make heads, but they need a lot of precious space.
- Spinach 'Red Cardinal' F1 and two orache at both ends of the row: spinach picked from mid April, abundant until flowering late May; lovely red orache leaves for salad from April to June.
- Fennel 'Zefa Fino' and a few antirrhinums: slugs ate all these seedlings.

Conclusions

The main period of harvests, from mid April, was perhaps a fortnight behind what one might expect in an average spring. A key factor is space needed for growth: smaller vegetables were the most productive, and the best harvests were from carrot, lettuce, spinach and coriander. Beetroot and peas grew well, but they have spreading leaves and either need wider rows, or you can grow taller, fast-cropping vegetables such as coriander, dill and radish in the row next to them.

The time and space needed for growing large vegetables, such as calabrese and cabbage, to maturity means they give little value in proportion to the work involved. Peas are viable from being more upright when supported; also nearby vegetables will have been harvested by the time they reach full size. Onions are economical with space, worth growing for both salad and early bulbs.

Hot bed 2

Growing bed: 1.2x2.4m (4x8'), made with 15cm (6") planks.
The base of this bed had a 1m (40") starting depth of fresh manure. In the cold spring it worked well, and the rapidly increasing day length and brighter sun throughout March meant fast growth after sowing and planting. Many of the vegetables were set out as 6-week-old plants.

Sowings, plantings and growing

All sowings and plantings were between 5 March and 8 March, at the same spacings as for hot bed 1, and also with some mixed and interplanted rows. By the morning of 9 March it was steamy under the fleece, in briefly calm, mild weather.

- Potato 'Swift' first early, two at either end: I barely saw any growth, and think that frost (not kept out by fleece at the edges) kept killing the young leaves. I then planted module-raised red lettuce Diveria in mid April.
- Pea 'Sugar Snap', module-raised plants: seven modules of three plants each gave pea shoots from early April until June; all new growing tips picked every week.

These photos were taken two weeks apart in April.

- Onion sets 'Stuttgarter': my idea was to have spring onions in April, but I allowed them to mature into lovely onions by early July, 4 weeks ahead of my main onions.
- Lettuce, mixed varieties, seven module-raised plants: excellent healthy growth, picked from early April to June, by which time overshadowed by onions.
- Beetroot 'Boltardy': some sown and some module-raised plants, regular twisting out of larger roots from early May and through June.
- Carrot 'Early Nantes': wonderful leaves but poor and pale roots; a bad batch of seed from Moles Seeds. Better harvests were from some radish 'French Breakfast', sown in the row at the same time as carrots, and pulled through late April.
- Spring onion 'White Lisbon', six modules of six seeds each: grew well, harvested by mid May.
- Pak choi, unknown variety: a few pickings in April of slug-eaten leaves, then they flowered.
- Spring onion 'White Lisbon', sown direct: good emergence, and I did not thin enough, so had masses of spindly salad onions in late May.
- Carrot 'Early Nantes': disappointing after they looked so good; again nice results from the intersowing of radish.
- Spinach 'Boa' F1: fine leaves from mid April to early June, picked individually when medium size.
- Carrot 'Adelaide' F1, 'Amsterdam Forcing': good flavour from both; small harvests in early May, bigger ones soon after.
- Radish 'Cherry Belle', multi-sown module plants: lovely radish, all picked by 20 April.
- Chard 'Rainbow', seven module-raised plants: planted in April, after no potatoes; picked small for salad leaves from late April.

Conclusions

The main differences between this and bed 1 were later sowing times, and using more module-raised plants. In both cases, harvests were as or almost as early, so a hot bed made in late February seems more worthwhile than one made in January. Lower light levels in the middle of winter slow growth, even if there is warmth below. Peas for shoots are worthwhile because regular picking keeps them a small size.

My difficulty with the Early Nantes carrots shows how seed choice is important, and I recommend Amsterdam Forcing for sowing on hot beds, as it has small leaves in proportion to root size. Potatoes are risky because the leaves must be protected from late frost, and also because of the space they need.

Second sowings and harvests

After all the early harvests, you have an emptying bed and summer is just beginning. So what next? The heat from below is only slight by now; just enough to help warmth-loving plants such as basil, cucurbits, tomatoes, melons and French beans. I was slow to take advantage of this, from allowing the first sowings to grow for a longer period of harvests.

Hot bed 1

Some of the bed was empty by late May, but the harvests of peas, lettuce and carrot continued throughout June. Straight after the last harvest of peas, on 2 July (later than usual, after the cold spring), I cut off the plants and set out 28 module-raised dwarf French beans 'La Victoire' in the middle. At either end I planted some leeks and sweet basil, between lettuce that were still cropping, and sowed some carrots between the beans.

The French beans were rampant in the hot summer and gave superb harvests through August, before trailing off and finishing by mid September (a trait of La Victoire, which is not the longest-cropping variety). So I removed the bean plants by cutting the stems at soil level, and found some

Early August: one squash plant on the further bed; French beans in the nearer bed.

of the carrots growing, small but worthwhile. Although partly eaten by maggots of carrot root fly from mid October, many continued growing through the mild December.

Basil was productive in August and September, and the Zermatt leeks were big by November. See opposite for comments on these results.

Hot bed 2

The deeper manure in this bed would have made it possible to grow melon, aubergine and pepper if I had set out decent-sized plants by early summer. In fact I planted just one 'Uchiki Kuri' winter squash, in a gap where spring onions had been harvested, and then I continued to harvest neighbouring spring vegetables as the squash plant began its climb over them. By early July its stems were running in all directions, and I had to push them to the edge for plantings on 2 July of celeriac 'Monarch', basil 'British', leek 'Bandit' and kale 'Cavolo Nero'.

Through August the abundant growth was lovely to see, with squash stems and leaves all around hot bed 1 as well. Finally, by early October, once all the leaves of this plant had died back, there were 13 squash averaging 1kg (2lb 3oz) each (pictured at the start of this chapter).

The other summer vegetables had suffered from their neighbour's vigour, causing a lack of light and moisture, except in the case of the basil, which I had picked regularly and kept clear of squash leaves. Then in October I was pleased to see leeks with no damage from leek moth caterpillars, which had been massacring some other leeks nearby. Perhaps this was from the hot bed leeks being hidden by squash leaves, or from

Early July: this is the 'Uchiki Kuri' squash plant.

plants being enclosed by pallets – by comparison, there was caterpillar damage to leeks on hot bed 1, which had a lower wooden surround. When I harvested the three roots of celeriac at Christmas, they weighed 1.6kg (3lb 8oz) altogether. There were still kale leaves to harvest, and the Bandit leeks needing to grow some more, but were running out of time.

Conclusions about summer vegetables on hot beds

By summer there is little residual heat in a hot bed. In July my thermometer showed temperatures only a little higher than in neighbouring soil. On the other hand, the fresh manure has begun to become compost, and its store of nutrients and moisture become more available to plants, hence the success of cucurbits in particular, which appreciate a long, rich root run.

The yield of squash from one plant was phenomenal, but the snag is how much eventual space and light are needed for growing. Melons and cucumbers are less invasive and worth trying in milder climates (zone 9 upwards), from plants raised under cover and set out by early summer. French beans grow well but are tricky to pick from plants in the middle of the bed!

Basil and leeks like hot beds, and tomatoes would too, but I did not try them because, as with any outdoor-grown tomatoes, they are at risk of blight from rain on the leaves, and again it would be hard to tend plants in the middle. You could grow aubergines and peppers in warmer climates; indeed there are lots of possible and interesting plants to try.

Disassembling and emptying

You can clear and empty both the growing bed and the base as soon as the last harvests are taken, usually before or early in winter. The contents provide compost for the garden, then you can start again with fresh manure.

Compost from the growing bed is fine, dark and crumbly, so could be used for potting, or as a mulch where you plan to sow small seeds such as carrots, or as a light surface covering for any bed. The manure is more variable, because it had to be squashed to create the bed, and a lack of air does not help decomposition. I found this more in the deeper manure of hot bed 2, which was still quite yellow in the middle with plenty of unrotted wood shavings. I spread it on flower beds and around apple trees.

Once everything is cleared away, you can build a new heap in the same space, or elsewhere. Hot beds are a thorough way of clearing ground!

I hope this chapter has given an idea of the work involved in using hot beds, which is significant, and some of the potential rewards. I am sure that you can discover others.

CHAPTER FIFTEEN

Perennial vegetables

A wider range of crops, complementary to annuals

"A garden is never so good as it will be next year."

Abraham Lincoln

Growing perennial vegetables is a different experience from the yearly cycle of growing annuals, and this chapter compares some advantages and disadvantages of each. To reap the full rewards of perennials, you need long-term commitment, to look after the plants and to keep harvesting too. Before making the decision to grow them, first check how suitable they are for the size of your plot, as well as for your growing

Sorrel, fruit bushes and kale in their second summer.

skills and inclinations, food needs and tastes, and the amount of time you have available. I suggest growing perennials in their own space, separate from a plot dedicated to annual sowings, which grow best in clear ground.

Pros and cons of perennial vegetables

As a contrast with perennials, I use the term 'annuals' for plants grown from seed which flower and die within 2 years. Although some have a biennial life cycle, in the case of vegetables the edible part grows in 1 year, so for our purposes they are treated as annuals.

Often, the question of whether to grow annual or perennial vegetables elicits answers that tend to favour one or the other. A better approach is to compare their individual merits and then grow a choice of both, for a wider range of food in all seasons, and in proportion to your available time and requirements for harvests.

Perennials do not need replanting every year

This is the main difference, and most others follow from it. Perennial plants survive winter, mostly dormant but not always, then grow strongly in spring with minimal input from the gardener. Asparagus and rhubarb can stay productive for over 20 years, globe artichokes for a little less, while perennial kale is more productive in new soil after 5 years.

However, this is not a no-work scenario. Most perennial vegetables need clearing of old stems, and thinning or dividing, either after cropping or at the end of each season – and occasionally they need replanting. Keeping the soil well mulched, and fed with compost too, helps to prolong the life of perennial plants.

Perennials require no soil preparation for planting each year

This is certainly true, but best results come from healthy soil with few weeds, so it is worth mulching with some organic matter, every autumn if possible. The increased growth and harvests, with fewer weeds too, repay the work involved.

However, perennial vegetables still need weeding. Even if you have an extensive forest garden (an established community of perennials at different heights, from ground cover to trees), weeds such as brambles, couch grass and stinging nettles can be invasive and reduce yields. It does not take as long to maintain clean soil around perennials as it does around annuals, so that no weeds are ever seeding or establishing, and this saves significant time in the long run.

Perennials can offer harvests in the hungry gap of spring

This is a key advantage; for example, there is food from asparagus, sorrel, kale, Welsh onion and rhubarb when many annual vegetables are still at

February: bed already planted, and I am adding compost.

seedling or small plant stage. However, perennial vegetables have less to offer in autumn and winter, with few edible roots in particular, suggesting that their role is complementary to, rather than a substitute for, annual vegetables. Also, overwintered vegetables grown from seed, such as broad beans, spinach, leeks and many salads, can crop early and help to bridge the hungry gap as well.

Perennials resist pests such as slugs

As established plants, the vigorous growth of perennials in spring is often strong enough to resist slugs and other pests too, in situations where small annual vegetables might be eaten. Perennial kale is so tall that rabbits cannot reach it.

However, perennial vegetables' shade for molluscs makes it difficult to succeed with sowings of annual vegetables nearby, because of slug damage to seedlings. This is one reason why it works better to have a patch of ground dedicated exclusively to annuals.

Perennials fit in with any larger planting schemes

A diverse range of plants growing all the time can, if well managed, lead to higher productivity from a given area, because their established root systems enable early growth in spring, and leaves at many levels can increase total photosynthesis. This is a theme in permaculture, the aim being to maximize the use of available light, warmth and moisture by having plants growing all the time.

However, in damp, high-latitude climates there is less abundance from mixed cropping, because of lower light levels, and perennial vegetables in a woodland or forest garden will yield less than those in full light. This may not be a problem, but it's good to be aware of this, and to research examples of mixed cropping in your climate zone, before planting.

Perennials can grow large and productive

This too is certainly true. However, the size of a plant rarely correlates with the yield of food to eat; for example, the yield of asparagus or globe artichoke is not high for the area needed by the plant. Also, perennial vegetables' large leaves and extensive root systems compete with nearby plants, to some distance in dry weather. So you need a fair amount of space to grow them well, and the yield per area is mostly average rather than high.

Perennials offer frequent and regular harvests

This is a great benefit, with cropping over many weeks from each plant, usually little and often rather than a glut. Perennial kale is my favourite for this as it gives food during much of the year.

Verdict?

So are perennial vegetables easier and more worthwhile to grow than annuals? The answer is "Yes and no!" A tricky part can be establishing plants, especially slow-growing ones such as asparagus. Doing a

April: asparagus seedlings in the greenhouse.

thorough job of clearing weeds before planting is important (see Chapter 4), even more than for annual vegetables, whose briefer tenure in the soil gives another chance, if needed, to clear perennial weeds after crops are finished.

The time required from planting to harvest is mostly greater with perennials. During the first year at Homeacres, I picked no rhubarb, globe artichokes or asparagus, because they were establishing for harvests in later years. If you want quick results in a new garden, annuals are more productive, and for fast and high yields of a great range of vegetables they offer more possibilities.

On the other hand, my perennial kale was a prolific leafy green vegetable only 5 months after planting, and gave huge yields all year long, from a relatively small area. Green leaves in late winter and spring are valuable, and this is one perennial harvest that can exceed the output of annuals as well as matching them for flavour. Other perennials for leaves are not as productive or delicious.

Growing perennial vegetables

The perennial vegetables described in this section are the most productive ones I know, of those suited to temperate climates. You can add fruits and nuts if you want to expand the planting possibilities. All of the photographs are from my new perennial plantings at Homeacres, made in compost on top of undisturbed pasture. The cost of the compost was more than paid for by the time saved in soil preparation and subsequent weeding, which has been slight, and the ground is now clear of all perennial weeds.

For such a high latitude the climate at Homeacres is kind, and with few extremes (see Chapter 1, page 22). Perennial plants take quick advantage of the mild conditions in winter to start growth from existing roots and tubers, giving earlier harvests than annual vegetables grown from seed in spring, and I find that a choice selection of perennials complements my annual crops well.

The spacings given in the table below are from plant to plant, in each direction, and can be used in beds. Or you can grow some of these plants in rows, but there is a snag – that their continually growing roots can take moisture and food from a fair distance. Hence they work well in blocks in beds, and also taller plants then offer each other support against wind.

Productive perennial vegetables – establishment and harvesting					
Vegetable	Sow	Plant	Spacing	First picking of new plants	Harvest period
Artichoke, globe	Spring or autumn	Late autumn, winter	90cm (36")	Year 2, summer	Late spring to summer
Artichoke, Jerusalem		Early spring	60cm (24")	Year 1, mid autumn	Autumn to spring
Artichoke, Chinese		Mid spring	45cm (18")	Year 1, mid autumn	Autumn
Asparagus	Early spring	Late winter	60cm (24")	Year 3, late spring	Late spring to early summer
Kale, perennial		Any time	60cm (24")	Year 1, spring	All year
Onion, Welsh & tree	Any time	Any time	30cm (12")	Year 1, early summer	Spring to autumn
Rhubarb	Spring	Late autumn	90cm (36")	Year 2, early spring	Spring to early summer
Sea kale	Spring or autumn	Spring	40cm (16")	Year 2, mid spring	Late spring
Sorrel	Any time	Any time	40cm (16")	Year 1, summer	Spring to autumn

February: globe artichoke in front; under the compost is undisturbed pasture.

Globe artichoke
(*Cynara cardunculus* Scolymus Group)

The main constraint is winter cold: in areas with frequent lows of -8°C (18°F) or colder, dormant plants should be covered with a loose mulch in early winter. New leaves appear in early spring, and growth is rapid until the first stems appear in midsummer, their flower buds pickable at any stage, depending on whether you want tender or more chunky leaf bases.

You can grow new plants from seed, but they are more genetically variable than from root division. To divide, use a sharp spade to cut roots of 10-15cm (4-6") length off the edges of existing plants in late autumn. I planted roots 1m (3') apart into a 10cm (4") mulch of old manure on pasture, then covered the bed with 5-7cm (2-3") of green-waste compost, after which the only weeding was to remove a few buttercups and dandelions trying to re-grow. I picked a few small artichokes in September, of a late-cropping variety, but the first year is mainly for establishment, whether grown from seed or roots.

For large gardens, cardoons (*Cynara cardunculus* Cardoon Group) are another possibility for their edible stems, and they do well in dry conditions, but the yield is low relative to the space required.

Jerusalem and Chinese artichoke
(*Helianthus tuberosus* and *Stachys affinis*)

Strictly speaking these are not perennials, because new plants start every spring from harvestable tubers, rather than from an enduring root system. However, new growth is so reliable and vigorous, with no disease problems, that established clumps can be allowed to become 'perennial'.

Jerusalem artichokes grow over 2m (6'6") high and are somewhat invasive, giving shade and taking moisture from nearby plants. Also, their tubers cause gas in the stomach, however you prepare them – I have tried many ways, from soups to salads.

Chinese artichokes, related to mint, have a mild and nutty flavour, but are small and fiddly to harvest. Their 60cm (24")-high foliage is frost-susceptible, so the planting date is later and harvesting earlier than for Jerusalem artichokes.

Asparagus
(*Asparagus officinalis*)

Asparagus is slow to establish, and it is wise to plant crowns into clean soil with no weeds or weed roots. If soil lies wet in winter, it is worth

1. Asparagus crowns planted into compost on undisturbed pasture. **2.** April: weeds pushing through; new cardboard laid. **3.** Hesitant growth by September. **4.** Mustard green manure in October (the mustard is growing in autumn only, when asparagus is becoming dormant).

raising the planting bed using soil from paths or extra compost to make a ridge for planting into. You can have a small harvest in the third spring, then every summer after solstice you stop picking and allow plants to grow large ferns, to recharge their roots.

Growing from seed works well if you can wait an extra year: I sowed some in March in the greenhouse and planted them in the gaps a year later, with good results as that had given time to clean the soil of all weeds. In year two when crowns and top growth are still only of medium size, you can intercrop with salads, peas, spinach, celery and any small-to-medium-sized vegetable, preferably planted in spring.

Kale
(*Brassica oleracea* var. *ramosa*)

Two common varieties of perennial kale are 'Taunton Deane' and 'Daubenton'. Both grow new leaves all year and rarely flower, hence it is hard to buy seed, and you need either to buy plants or to take a stem from a friend's plant. Propagation from stems is easy: just dib a hole in the soil or use a pot of compost, putting small stems in 5-10cm (2-4") deep with just two or three leaves showing above, at any time of year. Often they look dead for a while, then break out into leaf and turn into new plants.

These are branching plants, with many stems rather than one tall one. Each stem makes new leaves of medium size, which need frequent picking before they toughen or go yellow, or are eaten by insects. Being brassicas,

'Taunton Deane' kale 1 year from planting as small plants, and having been picked regularly.

they need protection from pigeons, but summer caterpillars rarely hurt the main plants and new growth keeps coming. The best harvests are from autumn to early winter, with slender pickings through any mild winter, until new growth is abundant in spring.

The leaves are tender and taste sweet – good in salads and smoothies, as well as blanched or stir-fried. Taunton Deane plants grow to 1.5m (5') high and spread out too. The rooting system is extensive, partly to anchor the tall plants in wind, and to feed all the new growth. I grew ten plants at Homeacres, and in the first year was picking leaves by April from a December planting, to supply the local wholefood shop with greens through a cold May, when they could find no other supply of leafy green vegetables.

Welsh onion and tree onion
(*Allium fistulosum* and *Allium cepa* Proliferum Group)

The Welsh onion – not from Wales but Asian in origin – is a common perennial. The name comes from old English 'welisc', meaning foreign. They are worth growing to have green onions for much of the year, except for a flowering period in summer, when they sport white flowers.

Tree onion, also called 'walking onion' and 'Egyptian onion', makes small bulbs instead of flowers, and sometimes the stems bend down under their weight, resulting in the bulbs rooting and making new plants (hence 'walking'). The bulbs and parental stems are strongly flavoured, the leaves being more chunky than Chinese chives (*Allium tuberosum*), whose main season of use is spring, until flowering.

Rhubarb
(*Rheum rhabarbarum*)

The flavour of rhubarb is refreshing, at a time when there are few fresh harvests. A trial by *Which? Gardening* in 2013 gave clear top marks, flavour-wise, to 'Valentine' and 'The Sutton'. A reliable variety is 'Timperley Early', with first pickings from late winter here, and without any forcing, which is necessary only if you want sweeter stems (bear in mind that forcing weakens the plant by light deprivation).

Plant as for globe artichoke (see page 237), leaving plants to grow unpicked in the first year after planting roots, or leave for 2 years after sowing seed. Thereafter it is best to stop picking in mid summer, so that plants can nourish their roots until leaves die back in autumn.

July: rhubarb, artichoke and kale after 7 months.

Sea kale
(*Crambe maritima*)

As the name suggests, this plant's native habitat is by the sea, and the best sea kale I know is where the gardener spread 7cm (3") of seaweed around and over plants in winter. His asparagus – also a sea vegetable – was equally prolific from the same treatment. An alternative is to spread seaweed meal and also some sea salt; a handful every square metre or square yard each year.

Grow plants either from seed, for a first harvest at least 2 years later, or from the roots of divided plants, to gain some time. The green leaves have a good flavour, and you get more harvests rather than from forcing for 2-3 weeks to have sweeter, yellow leaves in early spring, which slows subsequent growth.

Sorrel, broad-leaved and buckler-leaved
(*Rumex acetosa* and *Rumex scutatus*)

There are many variations of broad-leaved sorrel, including the wild, smaller-leaved sheep's sorrel (*Rumex acetosella*). All have lemon-tasting leaves that are great in soups and salads, and one clump of broad-leaved sorrel should give plenty of pickings – valuable in early spring when fresh greens are scarce. The flavour is astringent, and a common name is 'sour dock'. Grow either from seed or from divided roots, and when plants make flowering stems in early summer you can cut them to the ground to encourage more leaves. Also, there is a non-flowering version available as plants from certain suppliers. It is called Profusion® (*Rumex acetosa* 'TM683'), was developed by Richters, and grows large amounts of succulent, dark-green leaves.

Buckler-leaved sorrel is a smaller-yielding variation, grown in the same way, although seed is difficult to germinate and it is easier to transplant seedlings from self-seeding plants. In early spring there are many small leaves of delicate lemon flavour; less acidic than broad-leaved sorrel. Throughout summer it flowers, and you can cut stems close to the soil in late summer for more leaves in autumn.

Another common type is blood-veined sorrel (*Rumex sanguineus*, also known as 'bloody dock'!), whose leaves are decorative but with a bitter edge to the acidity.

Other perennial vegetables

There are many more perennial plants for food, of variable value, often with harvests of strong or unusual flavours that take some getting used to. Another way to broaden your palate is by foraging for hedgerow perennials, such as stinging nettles (*Urtica dioica*), for example. The following are just some of the many edible perennials that can be cultivated, or may be found growing wild.

Watercress (*Nasturtium officinale*) is normally grown in running water but can also be grown in soil, more as annual than a perennial, because it does not like frost – whereas in streams, plants are protected in freezing conditions by the higher temperature of water, at least around their roots. Sow in early spring, under cover if possible, to have pickings until flowering at midsummer, and then a few more leaves in autumn.

Sweet cicely (*Myrrhis odorata*) has a mild taste of aniseed and is excellent for sweetening dishes such as rhubarb or custard, and adding to bowls of salad. It is easier to divide a root for planting, rather than sowing seeds.

Skirret (*Sium sisarum*) is an umbellifer, grows up to 2m (6'6") high with flowers in summer, and has edible roots in winter. One of its colloquial names is 'witch's fingers', and that describes the multi-forking habit of its roots: although related to carrot and parsnip, they are less substantial. After harvesting, keep some root or roots to replant.

Good King Henry (*Chenopodium bonus-henricus*) has a taste of cucumber but dries the mouth and needs culinary skill to make it appealing, despite its other names of 'poor man's asparagus' and 'Lincolnshire spinach'. Again, it grows more reliably from divided roots than from seed.

One plant of skirret for roots.

Appendix: Seasons and climate zones

The table below translates months in the UK in terms of seasons, so that named months in this book can be easily interpreted by readers elsewhere.

January	Mid winter
February	Late winter
March	Early spring
April	Mid spring
May	Late spring
June	Early summer
July	Mid summer
August	Late summer
September	Early autumn
October	Mid autumn
November	Late autumn
December	Early winter

Please note that 'mid summer' is July – the middle of the summer growing season – whereas 'midsummer' in this book refers to late June, just after the summer solstice in the northern hemisphere.

Climate zones

Certain classifications exist for climatic ranges, as an indication of their suitability for plants of different hardiness.

The most commonly used system is the US Department of Agriculture (USDA) system of plant hardiness zones, which covers the full global range of temperatures: the hottest, zone 12b, is found in the tropics; the coldest, zone 1a, in the Arctic. This system has been widely adopted outside the USA. Most of the UK is in a climatic zone equivalent to USDA zones 8 and 9.

In the UK, the Royal Horticultural Society (RHS) uses a scale that is specific for the range of climates in the UK and northern Europe: from H1a (a heated greenhouse, equivalent to USDA zone 12b) to H7 (suitable only for very hardy plants, equivalent to USDA zone 6a).

Glossary

Annual plants grow from seed, then flower and set seed within the year. Examples include lettuce, radish and weeds such as bittercress and chickweed; some annuals, such as pea and broad (fava) bean, can overwinter as small plants, to grow and make seed the following summer.

Biennial plants grow from seed in their first year, overwinter as tuber, root or leafy plant, and then flower to set seed the following year. Examples include carrot and leek.

Blight, which usually refers to late blight (*Phytophthora infestans*), is a destructive fungus that can quickly kill tomato and potato plants in warm, wet weather. Dry leaves cannot be colonized by the fungal spores.

Cloches are low-level structures of polythene or glass, placed over plants to give protection from wind and some extra warmth.

Cold frames are low-level structures for protecting plants from wind, rain and low temperatures; their sides may be of wood, glass, plastic or brick, while their tops (called lights), which need lifting to ventilate plants in sunny weather, may be of glass or plastic.

Compaction of soil is caused by high pressure or cultivations when soil is vulnerable as a result of being wet and soft; in compacted soil, the growth of all plants is impeded. Adding organic matter and leaving soil undisturbed both reduce the likelihood of compaction, but if it happens, the recovery of soil structure takes time. Compacted soil is often grey or orange in pockets and streaks, and smells sulphurous from a lack of air and any flow of fresh water. See also 'firm soil'.

Compost is well-decomposed organic matter of dark colour and a more or less crumby texture, with a neutral or slightly pleasant smell. Different composts are described according to their original ingredients, for example green-waste compost (see 'municipal compost'), garden or home-made compost, or composted manure; or a previous use, for example mushroom compost; or a specific composting method, for example worm compost. There are also composts formulated with specific ingredients for sowing into ('seed compost') and potting – see 'multipurpose compost'.

Crop rotation is a term used to describe the approach of growing plants of different families in different places each year, often over a cycle of 4 years, so that in the fifth year they have 'rotated' back to the original place.

Damping off is when seedlings suddenly fall over and die from infection by mildew, caused by any or all of several factors: excessive moisture from overwatering, lack of ventilation, and too many seedlings close together.

Drainage refers to water passing through soil and then into aquifers or watercourses; good drainage means that water passes unheeded by any layers of high density, usually compaction, from soil being squashed or smeared while wet.

F1 hybrid seeds are raised from two inbred lines which are then cross-bred, sometimes using chemical stimulants, to give certain desired characteristics of growth. Saving seed from F1 varieties is not recommended, as the offspring grow 'out' to display less desirable characteristics (see also 'open-pollinated'). Incidentally, hybrid breeding has nothing to do with genetically modified (GM) seeds.

Families of plants are groups of several genera (see 'variety') which show similar patterns of growth and especially of flowering habit, for example the umbels of Umbelliferae (which have recently changed name to Apiaceae, as all plant family names now end in -aceae). Plants of the same family share many requirements for productive growth, but not all (different sowing dates, for example), and they are often susceptible to the same pests and diseases – a reason for crop rotation. The largest family of vegetables is the crucifers or Brassicaceae.

Fertility describes the ability of soil to grow healthy plants of worthwhile size, with reasonable drainage and water retention.

Fertilizer is plant food, and usually refers to a proprietary product, either water-soluble granules or liquid. Sometimes compost is wrongly referred to as fertilizer: its nutrients are insoluble in water, which means that they do not wash out in rain or from watering; in contrast, they become available through the interaction of soil life and plant roots, at suitable temperatures.

Firm soil has good structure, with air channels occupied by roots and by soil life such as fungi and worms; plants root well into firm soil, which is absolutely different from compacted soil.

Green-waste compost – see 'municipal compost'.

Growing medium refers to any materials into which plants can send their roots for nutrients and moisture. In this book the main types of growing medium are soil and compost.

Hardening off means giving plants that have been raised under cover a day or more of outdoor life while their roots are still undisturbed, in order to acclimatize them before planting out.

Hot beds are composed of fresh manures, including animal bedding and/or compost ingredients, which are still decomposing and therefore releasing heat. They are used for speeding growth, either of a bed of suitable growing medium placed on top of the heap, or of plants in trays positioned on a frame above the heap.

the Hungry gap refers to a month or two of spring when winter and stored vegetables have finished, but early sowings are not yet ready to harvest.

Leafmould is leaves that have been decomposing (usually piled up) for at least a year, sometimes longer, to turn dark and soft, often with some leaf shapes recognizable. As a compost it has less nutrient value than manure and home-made compost, but is excellent for mulching and as food for soil organisms.

Manure is animal excretions, and varies hugely in quality, according to: a) its age – it may be recent ('fresh') or old; b) which animals it came from; and c) which beddings were used, for example straw or wood shavings. When at least a year old and well stacked, manure becomes compost.

Mulch is a material laid on the soil surface to feed the soil, and/or to protect it from weather, and/or to exclude light from weeds. All three of these happen when compost and other organic matter is the mulch, and most plastic mulches achieve the last two.

Municipal compost is made in dedicated facilities from garden wastes mostly, in a hot process which kills weed seeds, pathogens and many organisms. Often there is a high content of shredded wood, and some plastic too: this may also be called 'green waste' compost. Some municipal and proprietary composts have food wastes added, which increases the nutrient supply. Check how finely the compost has been sieved; for garden use aim for 15mm (⅝") grade or less.

Multipurpose composts are proprietary products and include a broad range of mixes, based on either peat or composted waste of different kinds. They are suitable for sowing seeds, raising plants and re-potting, and can also be used as garden compost, although the quantities needed makes this an expensive option.

Nitrogen robbery describes weak plant growth where woody, carbon-rich ingredients of the soil's rooting zone are using some of the soil's available nitrogen for their decomposition, to the extent that plants grow more slowly and look pale.

No-dig means soil left undisturbed, apart from the initial and then occasional removal of some large, woody or deep-rooting weeds, light hoeing, and harvests of deep-rooted vegetables.

Nutrients are foods for plant growth, supplied either in man-made formulations (fertilizer) or by the addition of compost or other organic matter. Nutrients already present in soil can be made more available to plant roots by the addition of compost, owing to its effect of increasing microbial and fungal activity in the soil.

Open-pollinated seeds have grown outdoors and been pollinated by pollen in air or on insects, or from a flower applied by the gardener, and this wider spectrum of pollen qualities gives more variations in growth than from F1 hybrid breeding.

Organic is a term used for gardening and farming which focuses on feeding plants indirectly through feeding the soil, to achieve healthier growth with fewer pests and less disease.

Organic matter starts as plant residues, mostly leaves and stems, and is used in gardening at various stages of decomposition, sometimes after being eaten by animals (turned into manure) or worms too.

Perennial plants grow continually in some cases, or after dormancy in winter from food stored in their roots and tubers. Perennial weeds are the most persistent and difficult weeds to deal with. Perennial food plants need maintaining in the long term as opposed to re-sowing every year.

pH means acidity or alkalinity, and is often referred to in relation to soil acidity. Soil pH ranges from around 4.5 to 8.5, and outside these ranges growth is sparse. Soil with a pH below 7 is acid soil; above pH 7 is alkaline soil; and a pH from about 6.0 to 7.5 is fine for most plants. Most soils are within this range, so few gardens require any correction of soil pH, unless you want to grow plants with specific requirements, such as blueberries (acid-loving) and to a lesser extent brassicas, which prefer a fairly high pH.

Soil life is hugely varied, from bacteria and fungi to worms, beetles and spiders – all interacting and indescribably valuable for maintaining complex mechanisms of plant growth and decay.

Soil structure describes the matrix of crumbs within soil, which are held together by excretions of soil organisms after they have eaten organic matter, while air channels between and inside the crumbs maintain good drainage, moisture retention and healthy life for plant roots.

Subsoil is denser and lighter in colour than the topsoil above it. Roots use it, especially for moisture, but it is much less important to growth than topsoil.

Successional sowing is new sowings through the season, so that harvests are continuous, and also so that soil is always growing something. It is practised most in summer, when there are many possibilities for sowing to keep the plot full through autumn and into winter.

Topsoil is the biologically active and most nutrient-rich surface layer of soil, perhaps 20-25cm (8-10") deep, and recognizable by its darker colour than the subsoil below, which comes from the larger amount of organic matter it contains.

UV is ultraviolet light, which helps plants to produce anthocyanins, whose blue and red colours in food are associated with good health. One of the effects of UV light is to cause plastics to turn brittle.

Variety is the commonly used term for plant cultivar: plants within the same species which have been bred for different characteristics. So, for example, the carrot (*Daucus carota*), which is of family Apiaceae, is of genus *Daucus* and species *carota*: the species includes the wild carrot, and there are many varieties, of different maturity dates, length, flavour and colour.

Resources

The following (mainly UK) resources are ones that I use and warmly recommend. For readers in the USA, the web links on page 250 offer some useful starting points for further research.

Suppliers

The Backyard Larder
Contact by email only:
backyardlarder@tiscali.co.uk
www.backyardlarder.co.uk
Perennial plants by mail order.

Delfland Nurseries Ltd
Benwick Road, Doddington, March, Cambs PE15 0TU
Tel. 01354 740553
www.organicplants.co.uk
A range of plants available at all seasons.

Ferryman Polytunnels Ltd
Westleigh, Morchard Road, nr Crediton, Devon EX17 5LS
Tel. 01363 84948
www.ferrymanpolytunnels.co.uk
A wide range of polytunnels for sale, with installation on request.

Franchi Seeds
Available in the UK from: Seeds of Italy, D2 Phoenix Business Centre, Rosslyn Crescent, Harrow, Middx HA1 2SP
Tel. 020 8427 5020
www.seedsofitaly.com
Italian specialities such as tomato, chicory, endive and Florence fennel, and good-sized packets of most other vegetable seeds.

Implementations
PO Box 2568, Nuneaton CV10 9YR
Tel. 0845 330 3148
www.implementations.co.uk
Copper tools of quality and durability.

LBS Horticulture Ltd
Standroyd Mill, Cottontree, Colne, Lancs BB8 7BW
Tel. 01282 873370
www.lbsbuyersguide.co.uk
A good-value range of useful accessories, including netting, mesh, fleece, plug/ module trays and polytunnels.

The Organic Gardening Catalogue
Riverdene, Molesey Road, Hersham, Surrey KT12 4RG
Tel. 01932 253666
www.organiccatalogue.com
An extensive range of seeds and sundries.

The Real Seed Catalogue
PO Box 18, Newport, nr Fishguard, Pemb SA65 0AA
Tel. 01239 821107
www.realseeds.co.uk
A range of good, home-grown seeds and also advice on seed saving.

Richters Herb Specialists
357 Highway 47, Goodwood, ON L0C 1A0, Canada
(+1) 905 640 6677
www.richters.com
Plants and seeds, including Profusion® sorrel.

West Riding Organics Ltd
Halifax Road, Littleborough, Lancs OL15 0LF
Tel. 01706 379944
www.westridingorganics.co.uk
Potting composts based on peat sieved out of reservoirs.

www.quickcrop.co.uk/page/charles_dowding
A web page devoted to my 'essentials' collection – all kinds of useful materials and accessories.

And finally: for module/plug trays, B&Q (www.diy.com) sells sturdy, 60-cell trays, in packs of three.

Books and other publications

Back Garden Seed Saving: Keeping our vegetable heritage alive
Sue Stickland. eco-logic books, 2008.
Concise advice on how to save seeds in the garden from many common vegetables.

Charles Dowding's Veg Journal
Charles Dowding. Frances Lincoln, 2014.
A month-by-month look at the jobs for each time of year, to create and run a productive vegetable garden.

Charles Dowding's Vegetable Course
Charles Dowding. Frances Lincoln, 2012.
Covers all aspects of growing, with an emphasis on starting out, and includes chapters on weed identification.

Creating a Forest Garden: Working with nature to grow edible crops
Martin Crawford. Green Books, 2010.
A huge range of useful information, on the principles of forest gardening as well as a wealth of detail about crops, plus stunning photos.

The Fruit Tree Handbook
Ben Pike. Green Books, 2011.
All about fruit, from a professional grower: many good reviews show how useful this book is.

Gardening Myths and Misconceptions
Charles Dowding. Green Books, 2014.
Aimed at saving the reader time and money, this book explains the labour- and resource-demanding misunderstandings that are still common.

Hot Beds: How to grow early crops using an age-old technique
Jack First. Green Books, 2013.
How to make and sow hot beds: lots of practical advice based on long experience.

How to Grow Food in Your Polytunnel – All year round
Mark Gatter and Andy McKee. Green Books, 2010.
Ideas for planting under cover at different times of year. Advice on buying and erecting a tunnel can be found in The Polytunnel Handbook *by the same authors.*

How to Grow Perennial Vegetables: Low-maintenance, low-impact vegetable gardening
Martin Crawford. Green Books, 2012.
Wide-ranging subject matter, lots of good ideas and plenty of information on lesser-known as well as more common edible perennials.

How to Grow Winter Vegetables
Charles Dowding. Green Books, 2011.
For food all year round: this book actually covers much of the calendar year, from sowing in spring to harvesting in the hungry gap of spring!

How to Make and Use Compost: The ultimate guide
Nicky Scott. Green Books, 2009.
A distillation of the author's long and successful experience in making and using compost in many different ways.

Kitchen Garden magazine
www.kitchengarden.co.uk
Wide-ranging articles on vegetable growing, from many good writers.

The Maria Thun Biodynamic Calendar
Matthias Thun. Floris Books, published annually.
One of many calendars, this one concentrates on moon–constellation relationships.

Organic Gardening: The natural no-dig way
Charles Dowding. Green Books, 2007, 3rd edn 2013.
A best-seller, now in its third edition: covers most vegetables and some fruit too, with a first part that many readers say is like reading a bedtime novel!

The Polytunnel Book: Fruit and vegetables all year round
Joyce and Ben Russell. Frances Lincoln, 2011.
Sound advice on the basics and lots of good detail too, from an experienced couple.

Salad Leaves for All Seasons: Organic growing from pot to plot
Charles Dowding. Green Books, 2008.
A wealth of salad leaves explained, showing how you can grow more successfully when adapting your sowings to each season.

Teaming with Microbes: The organic gardener's guide to the soil food web
Jeff Lowenfels and Wayne Lewis. Timber Press, 2006, revised edn 2010.
An excellent explanation of soil life, in fact this book brings the subject matter alive too and is sure to enthuse you.

Teaming with Nutrients: The organic gardener's guide to optimizing plant nutrition
Jeff Lowenfels. Timber Press, 2013.
Follows from the above; an entertaining account of plants' feeding.

The Weeder's Digest: Identifying and enjoying edible weeds
Gail Harland. Green Books, 2012.
A valuable forager's guide so that you can find food more easily, with less walking!

Which? Gardening magazine
www.which.co.uk/magazine/gardening
Information and research into latest trends and proprietary products such as composts, tools and seeds.

Websites

www.rhs.org.uk
The Royal Horticultural Society. A rich resource of useful information on gardening.

www.charlesdowding.co.uk
My own website. Comprehensive information on vegetable growing; also dates of courses and open days at Homeacres.

Resources in the USA*

There are several websites offering recipes for mulching and creating a weed-free, no-dig garden. The following two examples both include links to further information.

www.no-dig-vegetablegarden.com/build-a-garden.html
Provides helpful information, albeit a little formulaic – I suggest you be prepared to improvise if all the suggested ingredients are not to hand.

www.treehugger.com/green-food/try-no-dig-gardening-for-your-backyard-vegetables.html
This blog also gives a recipe, although for me there is too much surface mulch, and it is noted that slugs soon appeared!

www.rodaleinc.com/brand/organic-gardening
For information on organic gardening, inspired by J. I. Rodale. Rodale's also publishes a monthly magazine, Organic Gardening.

www.soilfoodweb.com
Dr Elaine Ingham has pioneered many methods of increasing soil fertility.

These notes are available as a pdf with live hyperlinks at www.greenbooks.co.uk/htcanvg-usa-resources

Index

Also by Green Books

How to Grow Winter Vegetables

Charles Dowding

Enjoy an abundance of vegetables, even in the depths of winter.

Salad Leaves for All Seasons

Organic growing from pot to plot

Charles Dowding

Discover the secrets to keeping fresh, tasty salads on your table all year.

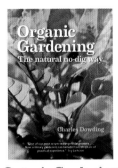

Organic Gardening

The natural no-dig way

Charles Dowding

The definitive guide to no-dig organic gardening.

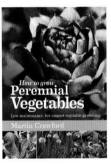

How to Grow Perennial Vegetables

Low-maintenance, low-impact vegetable gardening

Martin Crawford

Comprehensive advice on all types of perennial vegetables.

Creating a Forest Garden

Working with nature to grow edible crops

Martin Crawford

The forest garden 'bible' explains how to design, plant and maintain your plot.

Hot Beds

How to grow early crops using an age-old technique

Jack First

A handy guide to growing early crops, the organic way.

About Green Books

green books

Environmental publishers for 25 years. For our full range of titles and to order direct from our website, see: **www.greenbooks.co.uk**

Send us a book proposal on eco-building, science, gardening, etc.: see **www.greenbooks.co.uk/for-authors**

For bulk orders (50+ copies) we offer discount terms. For details, contact **sales@greenbooks.co.uk**

Join our mailing list for new titles, special offers, reviews and author events: **www.greenbooks.co.uk/subscribe**

 @ Green_Books   /GreenBooks